FARMHOUSE
FAMILY DINNERS

TASTE OF HOME BOOKS • RDA ENTHUSIAST BRANDS, LLC • MILWAUKEE, WI

ISBN: 978-1-62145-868-5
Component Number: 116700115H

Executive Editor: Mark Hagen
Senior Art Director: Raeann Thompson
Assistant Editor: Sammi DiVito
Art Director: Maggie Conners
Deputy Editor, Copy Desk: Dulcie Shoener
Copy Editor: Kara Dennison
Contributing Designer: Jennifer Ruetz

Cover
Photographer: Mark Derse
Set Stylist: Melissa Franco
Food Stylist: Shannon Norris

Pictured on title page: Balsamic Braised Pot Roast, p. 57

Pictured on back cover: Red, White & Blue Summer Salad, p. 75; Beef
Tenderloin with Roasted Vegetables, p. 67; Smoky Macaroni & Cheese, p. 89

Printed in China
1 3 5 7 9 10 8 6 4 2

MORE WAYS TO CONNECT WITH US:

Cover Meal

- Citrus-Herb Roast Chicken, p. 71
- Chive Smashed Potatoes, p. 78
- Garden Chickpea Salad, p. 84
- Easy Batter Rolls, p. 76
- Strawberry Mascarpone Cake, p. 105

SERVE WITH: Dutch-Oven Bread, Page 85

CONTENTS

CHAPTER 1: FARMHOUSE MENUS 4

CHAPTER 2: ONE-DISH SUNDAY DINNERS 46

CHAPTER 3: FAVORITE FARMHOUSE ENTREES 58

CHAPTER 4: COUNTRY SIDES, SALADS & MORE 72

CHAPTER 5: TASTY ODDS & ENDS 86

CHAPTER 6: MEMORY-MAKING DESSERTS 98

CHAPTER 1
FARMHOUSE MENUS

The dinner table is a place to relax, regroup and reconnect. After all, few things bring families together like sharing a home-cooked meal at the end of the day. Here, you'll find 10 complete dinners ideal for weeknights, Sunday dinners and special occasions alike. Prepare one tonight, then settle in for the heartwarming comfort best found when surrounded by those you love most.

Hearty Ham Dinner

- Maple-Glazed Ham
- Citrus-Tarragon Asparagus Salad
- Overnight Yeast Rolls
- Refreshing Raspberry Iced Tea
- Chocolate & Coconut Cream Torte

MAPLE-GLAZED HAM

MAPLE-GLAZED HAM

I cook this ham for Christmas and Easter, but my husband thinks that twice a year is not enough. If it were up to him, we'd eat this every day! When I have larger hams, I double the glaze, which is also good on pancakes the next day.

—*Jeanie Beasley, Tupelo, MS*

PREP: 10 MIN. • **COOK:** 1¾ HOURS
MAKES: 15 SERVINGS

- 1 spiral-sliced fully cooked bone-in ham (7 to 9 lbs.)

GLAZE
- ½ cup packed brown sugar
- ½ cup maple syrup
- 2 Tbsp. prepared mustard
- ½ tsp. ground cinnamon
- ¼ tsp. ground nutmeg

1. Preheat oven to 300°. Place ham on a rack in a shallow roasting pan. Cover and bake until a thermometer reads 130°, 1½ to 2 hours.
2. Meanwhile, in a large saucepan, combine glaze ingredients. Bring to a boil; cook and stir until slightly thickened, 2-3 minutes.
3. Remove the ham from oven. Pour maple glaze over the ham. Bake ham, uncovered, until a thermometer reads 140°, 15-30 minutes longer.
4 oz.: 234 cal., 6g fat (2g sat. fat), 93mg chol., 1137mg sod., 15g carb. (14g sugars, 0 fiber), 31g pro.

KITCHEN TIP: Have a lot of leftovers? Ham stores very nicely in the freezer. Just be sure to use it up within 4 months for the best flavor and texture.

CITRUS-TARRAGON ASPARAGUS SALAD

CITRUS-TARRAGON ASPARAGUS SALAD

I created this colorful salad when I was invited to a friend's Easter egg hunt and potluck picnic. The guests took one bite and were begging to get my recipe. My advice is to try to let the flavors infuse overnight for the best taste.

—*Cheryl Magnuson, Apple Valley, CA*

PREP: 40 MIN. + CHILLING • **BROIL:** 15 MIN.
MAKES: 12 SERVINGS

- 3 medium sweet red peppers
- 3 lbs. fresh asparagus, trimmed
- ½ cup minced shallots

DRESSING
- ⅓ cup white balsamic vinegar
- 2 Tbsp. grated orange zest
- 2 Tbsp. minced fresh tarragon
- 1 Tbsp. honey
- 1 tsp. sea salt
- ¼ tsp. pepper
- ⅔ cup walnut or olive oil

1. Preheat broiler. Place peppers on a foil-lined baking sheet. Broil 4 in. from heat until skins blister, about 5 minutes. With tongs, rotate peppers a quarter turn. Broil and rotate until all sides are blistered and blackened. Immediately place peppers in a large bowl; let stand, covered, 20 minutes.
2. Meanwhile, in a 6-qt. stockpot, bring 8 cups water to a boil. Add asparagus in batches; cook, uncovered, just until crisp-tender, 1-2 minutes. Remove the asparagus and immediately drop into ice water. Drain and pat dry; cut into halves.
3. Peel off and discard charred skin on peppers. Remove stems and seeds. Cut peppers into ¼-in.-wide strips. In a large bowl, combine asparagus, red peppers and shallots. For dressing, in a small bowl, whisk the vinegar, orange zest, tarragon, honey, salt and pepper. Gradually whisk in oil until blended. Drizzle over the asparagus mixture; toss to coat. Refrigerate up to 4 hours before serving, stirring occasionally.
¾ cup: 148 cal., 12g fat (1g sat. fat), 0mg chol., 168mg sod., 9g carb. (6g sugars, 2 fiber), 2g pro. **Diabetic exchanges:** 2½ fat, 1 vegetable.

OVERNIGHT YEAST ROLLS

It's easy to make light and flavorful rolls with this no-fuss recipe. The dough can also be used for cinnamon rolls, herb bread or coffee cake.
—*Trisha Kruse, Eagle, ID*

PREP: 20 MIN. + CHILLING • **BAKE:** 15 MIN.
MAKES: 2 DOZEN

- 1 Tbsp. sugar
- 1 Tbsp. active dry yeast
- 1½ tsp. salt
- 5½ to 6 cups all-purpose flour
- 1 cup buttermilk
- ½ cup water
- ½ cup butter, cubed
- 3 large eggs, room temperature
- 2 Tbsp. butter, melted

1. In a large bowl, mix sugar, yeast, salt and 3 cups flour. In a small saucepan, heat buttermilk, water and ½ cup butter to 120°-130°. Add to dry ingredients; beat on medium speed 2 minutes. Add the eggs; beat on high 2 minutes. Stir in enough remaining flour to form a soft dough (dough will be sticky).
2. Do not knead. Place the dough in a large greased bowl. Cover and refrigerate overnight.
3. Punch down dough. Turn onto a lightly floured surface; divide and shape into 24 balls. Place 2 in. apart on greased baking sheets. Cover with kitchen towels; let rise in a warm place until almost doubled, about 1½ hours.
4. Preheat oven to 400°. Bake until golden brown, 15-20 minutes. Brush with melted butter. Remove from pans to wire racks; serve warm.
1 roll: 163 cal., 6g fat (3g sat. fat), 36mg chol., 215mg sod., 23g carb. (1g sugars, 1g fiber), 4g pro.

REFRESHING RASPBERRY ICED TEA

This recipe makes two gallons, so it's a sensible thirst-quenching choice for a springtime party when you have a medium-size crowd. It also freezes well, a timesaver for party prep.
—*Arlana Hendricks, Manchester, TN*

PREP/TOTAL: 20 MIN. • **MAKES:** 16 SERVINGS

- 6 cups water
- 1¾ cups sugar
- 8 tea bags
- ¾ cup frozen apple-raspberry juice concentrate
- 8 cups cold water
  Ice cubes
  Fresh raspberries, optional

In a large saucepan, bring 6 cups water and sugar to a boil; remove from heat. Add the tea bags; steep, covered, for 3-5 minutes according to taste. Discard tea bags. Add the juice concentrate; stir in cold water. Serve over ice, with raspberries if desired.
1 cup: 108 cal., 0 fat (0 sat. fat), 0 chol., 7mg sod., 28g carb. (27g sugars, 0 fiber), 0 pro.

CHOCOLATE & COCONUT CREAM TORTE

My grandmother passed this recipe down to me years ago and now I make it for my own grandchildren. When preparing, make sure the chocolate layer is properly chilled before adding the next layer, or the coconut will sink into it.
—*Jason Purkey, Ocean City, MD*

PREP: 25 MIN. + CHILLING
COOK: 10 MIN. + STANDING
MAKES: 12 SERVINGS

- 1 pkg. (12 oz.) vanilla wafers, crushed
- ½ cup butter, melted
- 8 oz. dark baking chocolate, chopped
- 1 cup heavy whipping cream
FILLING
- 1 can (13½ oz.) coconut milk
- 3 cups sweetened shredded coconut
- 1 cup sugar
- 2 Tbsp. cornstarch
- 4 Tbsp. cold water, divided
- 1 large egg
- 1 large egg yolk
- 2 tsp. unflavored gelatin
- 1¼ cups heavy whipping cream
- ½ cup sweetened shredded coconut, toasted

1. In a large bowl, mix wafer crumbs and butter. Press onto bottom and 2 in. up side of a greased 9-in. springform pan.
2. Place chocolate in a small bowl. In a small saucepan, bring 1 cup cream just to a boil. Pour over chocolate; let stand 5 minutes. Stir with a whisk until smooth. Pour over prepared crust. Refrigerate for 1 hour.
3. In a large saucepan, combine coconut milk, coconut and sugar; bring just to a boil. Strain through a fine-mesh strainer into a bowl, reserving strained coconut; return the coconut milk mixture to the saucepan. In a bowl, mix cornstarch and 2 Tbsp. water until smooth; stir into coconut milk mixture. Return to a boil, stirring constantly; cook and stir until thickened, 1-2 minutes. Remove from the heat.
4. In a small bowl, whisk egg and egg yolk. Whisk a small amount of hot mixture into egg mixture; return all to pan, whisking constantly. Bring to a gentle boil; cook and stir 2 minutes. Remove from heat.
5. In a microwave-safe bowl, sprinkle gelatin over remaining 2 Tbsp. cold water; let stand 1 minute. Microwave on high for 30-40 seconds. Stir and let stand until the gelatin is completely dissolved, 1 minute. Whisk gelatin mixture into coconut milk mixture. Refrigerate, covered, 1 hour, whisking every 15 minutes.
6. In a large bowl, beat cream until stiff peaks form; fold into coconut milk mixture. Spoon reserved strained coconut into prepared crust. Spread filling over coconut. Refrigerate for 6 hours or overnight before serving.
7. Remove rim from pan. Top with toasted coconut.
1 piece: 691 cal., 49g fat (32g sat. fat), 107mg chol., 265mg sod., 63g carb. (49g sugars, 3g fiber), 6g pro.

CHOCOLATE &
COCONUT CREAM TORTE

Fried-Chicken Sunday Dinner

- Best-Ever Fried Chicken
- Traditional Mashed Potatoes
- Kale Caesar Salad
- Southern Buttermilk Biscuits

BEST-EVER FRIED CHICKEN

BEST-EVER FRIED CHICKEN

I grew up on a farm, and every year when it was time to bale hay, my dad would hire farm hands to help out. The crew looked forward to coming because they knew that they would be treated to my mom's delicious fried chicken.
—*Lola Clifton, Vinton, VA*

PREP: 15 MIN. • **COOK:** 20 MIN.
MAKES: 4 SERVINGS

1¾   cups all-purpose flour
1   Tbsp. dried thyme
1   Tbsp. paprika
2   tsp. salt
2   tsp. garlic powder
1   tsp. pepper
1   large egg
⅓   cup whole milk
2   Tbsp. lemon juice
1   broiler/fryer chicken (3 to 4 lbs.), cut up
     Oil for deep-fat frying

1. In a shallow bowl, mix the first 6 ingredients. In a separate shallow bowl, whisk the egg, milk and lemon juice until blended. Dip chicken in flour mixture to coat all sides; shake off excess. Dip in egg mixture, then again in flour mixture.
2. In an electric skillet or deep fryer, heat oil to 375°. Fry the chicken, a few pieces at a time, until golden brown and chicken juices run clear, 6-10 minutes on each side. Drain on paper towels.
1 serving: 811 cal., 57g fat (9g sat. fat), 176mg chol., 725mg sod., 26g carb. (2g sugars, 2g fiber), 47g pro.

KITCHEN TIP: To get crispy skin on fried chicken, it's important to remove extra moisture from the chicken before dredging. Refrigerating the dredged chicken before cooking can also help.

SOUTHERN BUTTERMILK BISCUITS

KALE CAESAR SALAD

I love Caesar salad recipes, so I created this version with kale. It's perfect paired with chicken or steak for a family meal.
—*Rashanda Cobbins, Milwaukee, Wisconsin*

TAKES: 15 MIN. • **MAKES:** 8 SERVINGS

- 4　cups chopped fresh kale
- 4　cups torn romaine
- 1　cup Caesar salad croutons
- ½　cup shredded Parmesan cheese
- ½　cup mayonnaise
- 2　Tbsp. lemon juice
- 1　Tbsp. Worcestershire sauce
- 2　tsp. Dijon mustard
- 2　tsp. anchovy paste
- 1　garlic clove, minced
- ¼　tsp. salt
- ¼　tsp. pepper

In a large salad bowl, toss the kale, romaine, croutons and cheese. For dressing, combine remaining ingredients in a small bowl; pour over salad and toss to coat. Serve salad immediately.
1 cup: 148 cal., 13g fat (3g sat. fat), 10mg chol., 417mg sod., 6g carb., (1g sugars, 1g fiber), 3g. **Diabetic exchanges:** 2½ fat, 1 vegetable.

TRADITIONAL MASHED POTATOES

Mashed potatoes go with just about any meal, so I keep this recipe handy. I like to use good ol' russets or Yukon Golds.
—Taste of Home *Test Kitchen*

TAKES: 30 MIN.
MAKES: 6 SERVINGS (ABOUT 4½ CUPS)

- 6　medium russet potatoes (about 2 lbs.), peeled and cubed
- ½　cup warm whole milk or heavy whipping cream
- ¼　cup butter, cubed
- ¾　tsp. salt
　　Dash pepper

Place potatoes in a large saucepan; add water to cover. Bring to a boil. Reduce heat to medium; cook, uncovered, until very tender (easily pierced with a fork), 20-25 minutes. Drain. Add remaining ingredients; mash until light and fluffy.
¾ cup: 168 cal., 8g fat (5g sat. fat), 22mg chol., 367mg sod., 22g carb. (3g sugars, 1g fiber), 3g pro.

SOUTHERN BUTTERMILK BISCUITS

The recipe for these four-ingredient biscuits has been handed down for many generations.
—*Fran Thompson, Tarboro, NC*

TAKES: 30 MIN. • **MAKES:** 8 BISCUITS

- ½　cup cold butter, cubed
- 2　cups self-rising flour
- ¾　cup buttermilk
　　Melted butter

1. In a large bowl, cut butter into flour until mixture resembles coarse crumbs. Stir in buttermilk just until moistened. Turn onto a lightly floured surface; knead 3-4 times. Pat or lightly roll to ¾-in. thickness. Cut with a floured 2½-in. biscuit cutter.
2. Place on a greased baking sheet. Bake at 425° until golden brown, 11-13 minutes. Brush tops with butter. Serve warm.
1 biscuit: 222 cal., 12g fat (7g sat. fat), 31mg chol., 508mg sod., 24g carb. (1g sugars, 1g fiber), 4g pro.

TRADITIONAL
MASHED POTATOES

Farmhouse Turkey

- Juicy Roast Turkey
- Moist Turkey Sausage Stuffing
- Almond Broccoli Salad
- Southern Sweet Potato Tart

JUICY
ROAST
TURKEY

JUICY ROAST TURKEY

I can't wait to serve this juicy turkey at Thanksgiving—so I make it several times a year. The aroma that wafts through the house during baking is almost as mouthwatering as the turkey itself.
—*Terrie Herman, North Myrtle Beach, SC*

PREP: 20 MIN. + CHILLING
BAKE: 3½ HOURS + STANDING
MAKES: 12 SERVINGS

- ¼ cup ground mustard
- 2 Tbsp. Worcestershire sauce
- 2 Tbsp. olive oil
- ½ tsp. white vinegar
- 1 tsp. salt
- ⅛ tsp. pepper
- 1 turkey (10 to 12 lbs.)
- 1 medium onion, quartered
- 2 celery ribs, quartered lengthwise
  Fresh parsley sprigs
- 2 bacon strips
- ¼ cup butter, softened
- 2 cups chicken broth
- 1 cup water

1. In a small bowl, combine the first 6 ingredients. Brush over the turkey. Place turkey on a platter. Cover and refrigerate for 1-24 hours.
2. Preheat oven to 325°. Place turkey on a rack in a shallow roasting pan, breast side up. Add the onion, celery and parsley to turkey cavity. Tuck wings under turkey; tie drumsticks together. Arrange bacon over top of turkey breast. Spread butter over turkey. Pour broth and water into pan.
3. Bake, uncovered, until a thermometer inserted in thickest part of thigh reads 170°-175°, 3½ to 4 hours, basting occasionally. Remove turkey from oven. If desired, remove and discard bacon. Tent with foil; let stand 20 minutes before carving. If desired, skim fat and thicken pan drippings for gravy. Serve with turkey.
8 oz. cooked turkey: 535 cal., 29g fat (9g sat. fat), 219mg chol., 594mg sod., 2g carb. (1g sugars, 0 fiber), 62g pro.

MOIST TURKEY
SAUSAGE STUFFING

MOIST TURKEY SAUSAGE STUFFING

With tangy apricots and hearty turkey sausage, this stuffing is a terrific mix of sweet and savory.
—*Priscilla Gilbert, Indian Harbour Beach, FL*

PREP: 20 MIN. • **COOK:** 20 MIN.
MAKES: 16 SERVINGS

- 1 pkg. (19½ oz.) Italian turkey sausage links, casings removed
- 4 celery ribs, chopped
- 1 large onion, chopped
- 1½ cups chopped dried apricots
- ¼ cup minced fresh parsley
- 1 Tbsp. minced fresh sage or 1 tsp. dried sage
- 1 tsp. poultry seasoning
- ¼ tsp. pepper
- 3¼ cups chicken stock
- 1 pkg. (12 oz.) crushed cornbread stuffing
- 1 cup fresh or frozen cranberries, chopped

1. In a Dutch oven, cook the turkey sausage, celery and onion over medium heat until meat is no longer pink and vegetables are tender, breaking sausage into crumbles; drain. Stir in the apricots, parsley, sage, poultry seasoning and pepper; cook 3 minutes longer.
2. Add stock; bring to a boil. Stir in cornbread stuffing; cook and stir until liquid is absorbed. Gently stir in the cranberries; heat through.
⅔ cup: 176 cal., 3g fat (1g sat. fat), 13mg chol., 540mg sod., 30g carb. (8g sugars, 3g fiber), 7g pro. **Diabetic exchanges:** 2 starch, 1 lean meat.

ALMOND
BROCCOLI SALAD

SOUTHERN SWEET POTATO TART

We love sweet potatoes, so I try to add them to as many dishes as I can. My tart secret ingredient is bourbon—it's what makes it so delicious.
—*Marie Bruno, Watkinsville, GA*

PREP: 1 HOUR • **BAKE:** 25 MIN. + COOLING
MAKES: 8 SERVINGS

- 1 lb. sweet potatoes (about 2 small) Pastry for single-crust pie
- ¼ cup butter, softened
- ½ cup packed dark brown sugar
- 2 Tbsp. all-purpose flour
- 1 tsp. pumpkin pie spice
- ¼ tsp. salt
- 1 large egg
- ¼ cup heavy whipping cream
- 1 Tbsp. bourbon or 1 Tbsp. whipping cream plus ½ tsp. vanilla extract

TOPPING
- 2 Tbsp. butter, softened
- 2 Tbsp. dark brown sugar
- 2 Tbsp. dark corn syrup
- ½ cup chopped pecans

1. Preheat oven to 400°. Place potatoes on a foil-lined baking sheet. Bake until tender, 40-50 minutes.
2. On a lightly floured surface, roll dough to a ⅛-in.-thick circle; transfer to a 9-in. tart pan with removable bottom. Press onto bottom and up side of pan; trim the edges to edge of pan. Refrigerate while preparing filling.
3. Remove potatoes from oven; increase oven setting to 425°. When potatoes are cool enough to handle, remove peel and place pulp in a large bowl; beat until smooth (you will need 1 cup mashed). Add butter, brown sugar, flour, pie spice and salt; beat until blended. Beat in egg, cream and bourbon. Pour into crust. Bake on a lower oven rack 15 minutes.
4. Meanwhile, for topping, mix butter, brown sugar and corn syrup until blended. Stir in pecans.
5. Remove pie; reduce oven setting to 350°. Spoon topping evenly over pie. Bake until a knife inserted in the center comes out clean, 8-10 minutes.
6. Cool on a wire rack. Serve within 2 hours or refrigerate, covered, and serve cold.
1 piece: 477 cal., 29g fat (15g sat. fat), 85mg chol., 326mg sod., 52g carb. (27g sugars, 3g fiber), 5g pro.

ALMOND BROCCOLI SALAD

This colorful salad is easy to make, and I like that it can be made ahead. Add the almonds and bacon just before serving so they stay nice and crunchy.
—*Margaret Garbade, Tulsa, OK*

TAKES: 25 MIN. • **MAKES:** 12 SERVINGS

- 1 bunch broccoli (about 1½ lbs.)
- 1 cup mayonnaise
- ¼ cup red wine vinegar
- 2 Tbsp. sugar
- ¼ tsp. salt
- ½ tsp. freshly ground pepper
- 1 pkg. (7 oz.) mixed dried fruit
- ¼ cup finely chopped red onion
- 1 pkg. (2¼ oz.) slivered almonds, toasted
- 4 bacon strips, cooked and crumbled

1. Cut florets from broccoli, reserving stalks; cut florets into 1-in. pieces. Using a paring knife, remove peel from thick stalks; cut stalks into ½-in. pieces.
2. In a small bowl, mix mayonnaise, vinegar, sugar, salt and pepper. In a large bowl, combine broccoli, dried fruit and onion. Add mayonnaise mixture; toss to coat. Refrigerate until serving.
3. Just before serving, sprinkle with almonds and bacon.
¾ cup: 236 cal., 17g fat (3g sat. fat), 1mg chol., 180mg sod., 21g carb. (15g sugars, 3g fiber), 3g pro.

SOUTHERN
SWEET POTATO
TART

Soup & Salad Supper

- Broccoli Beer Cheese Soup
- Roasted Apple Salad with Spicy Maple-Cider Vinaigrette
- Caraway Cheese Bread
- Autumn Apple Torte

BROCCOLI BEER CHEESE SOUP

BROCCOLI BEER CHEESE SOUP

Whether you include the beer or not, this soup tastes wonderful. I always make extra and pop individual servings into the freezer for fast meals.
—*Lori Lee, Brooksville, FL*

PREP: 20 MIN. • **COOK:** 30 MIN.
MAKES: 10 SERVINGS (2½ QT.)

3 Tbsp. butter
5 celery ribs, finely chopped
3 medium carrots, finely chopped
1 small onion, finely chopped
4 cups fresh broccoli florets, chopped
¼ cup chopped sweet red pepper
4 cans (14½ oz. each) chicken broth
½ tsp. pepper
½ cup all-purpose flour
½ cup water
3 cups shredded cheddar cheese
1 pkg. (8 oz.) cream cheese, cubed
1 bottle (12 oz.) beer or nonalcoholic beer
Optional toppings: Additional shredded cheddar cheese, cooked and crumbled bacon strips, chopped green onions, sour cream and salad croutons

1. In a Dutch oven, melt butter over medium-high heat. Add celery, carrots and onion; saute until crisp-tender. Add broccoli and red pepper; stir in broth and pepper. Combine flour and water until smooth; gradually stir into pan. Bring to a boil. Reduce heat; simmer, uncovered, until soup is thickened and vegetables are tender, 25-30 minutes.
2. Stir in cheeses and beer until cheeses are melted (do not boil). Top with additional shredded cheese, bacon, green onions, sour cream and croutons as desired.
FREEZE OPTION: Before adding toppings, cool soup; transfer to freezer containers. Freeze up to 3 months. To use, partially thaw in refrigerator overnight; heat through in a large saucepan over medium-low heat, stirring occasionally (do not boil). Add toppings as desired.
1 cup: 316 cal., 23g fat (13g sat. fat), 69mg chol., 1068mg sod., 13g carb. (5g sugars, 2g fiber), 12g pro.

ROASTED APPLE SALAD WITH SPICY MAPLE-CIDER VINAIGRETTE

ROASTED APPLE SALAD WITH SPICY MAPLE-CIDER VINAIGRETTE

We bought loads of apples and needed to use them. To help the flavors come alive, I roasted the apples and tossed them with a sweet dressing.
—*Janice Elder, Charlotte, NC*

PREP: 15 MIN. • **BAKE:** 20 MIN. + COOLING
MAKES: 8 SERVINGS

4 medium Fuji, Gala or other firm apples, quartered
2 Tbsp. olive oil
DRESSING
2 Tbsp. cider vinegar
2 Tbsp. olive oil
1 Tbsp. maple syrup
1 tsp. Sriracha chili sauce
½ tsp. salt
¼ tsp. pepper
SALAD
1 pkg. (5 oz.) spring mix salad greens
4 pitted dates, quartered
1 log (4 oz.) fresh goat cheese, crumbled
½ cup chopped pecans, toasted

1. Preheat oven to 375°. Place apples in a foil-lined 15x10x1-in. baking pan; drizzle with oil and toss to coat. Roast apples until tender, 20-30 minutes, stirring occasionally. Cool completely.
2. In a small bowl, whisk dressing ingredients until blended. In a large bowl, combine salad greens and dates. Drizzle dressing over salad and toss to coat.
3. Divide mixture among eight plates. Top with goat cheese and roasted apples; sprinkle with pecans. Serve immediately.
1 cup: 191 cal., 13g fat (3g sat. fat), 9mg chol., 240mg sod., 17g carb. (12g sugars, 3g fiber), 3g pro. **Diabetic exchanges:** 2 fat, 1 vegetable, ½ fruit.

CARAWAY CHEESE BREAD

AUTUMN APPLE TORTE

When it's apple season, we always make room for a slice of this heartwarming torte. It features a cream cheese layer and apples galore.
—*Margaret Wilson, San Bernardino, CA*

PREP: 40 MIN. • **BAKE:** 35 MIN. + COOLING
MAKES: 12 SERVINGS

- ½ cup butter, softened
- ½ cup sugar, divided
- ½ tsp. vanilla extract
- 1 cup all-purpose flour
- 1 pkg. (8 oz.) cream cheese, softened
- 1 large egg, room temperature, lightly beaten
- ½ tsp. almond extract
- 2 cups thinly sliced, peeled Granny Smith apples (about 2 medium)
- 2 cups thinly sliced, peeled Cortland apples (about 2 medium)
- ¼ cup cinnamon sugar
- ¼ tsp. ground nutmeg
- ½ cup confectioners' sugar
- 2 Tbsp. 2% milk
- 2 Tbsp. sliced almonds, toasted

1. Preheat oven to 450°. In a small bowl, cream butter and ¼ cup sugar until light and fluffy, 5-7 minutes. Beat in vanilla. Gradually beat in flour. Press onto bottom and 1 in. up side of a greased 9-in. springform pan.
2. In a small bowl, beat cream cheese and remaining sugar until smooth. Add egg and almond extract; beat on low speed just until blended. Pour into crust.
3. Place apples in a large bowl. Mix cinnamon sugar and nutmeg; add to apples and toss to coat. Arrange over cream cheese mixture. Bake 5 minutes.
4. Reduce oven setting to 400°. Bake until apples are tender, 30-35 minutes longer. Cool on a wire rack.
5. Remove rim from pan. In a small bowl, mix confectioners' sugar and milk until smooth. Drizzle over torte; sprinkle with almonds. Refrigerate leftovers.
1 piece: 270 cal., 15g fat (9g sat. fat), 57mg chol., 136mg sod., 31g carb. (22g sugars, 1g fiber), 3g pro.

CARAWAY CHEESE BREAD

We enjoy cheese in a variety of ways. In this savory bread, cheddar cheese blends beautifully with just the right amount of caraway and Dijon.
—*Homer Wooten, Ridgetown, ON*

PREP: 10 MIN. • **BAKE:** 30 MIN. + COOLING
MAKES: 1 LOAF (16 SLICES)

- 2½ cups all-purpose flour
- 2 cups shredded cheddar cheese
- 1½ to 2 tsp. caraway seeds
- ¾ tsp. salt
- ½ tsp. baking powder
- ½ tsp. baking soda
- 2 large eggs, room temperature
- 1 cup plain yogurt
- ½ cup butter, melted
- 1 Tbsp. Dijon mustard

1. Preheat oven to 375°. In a large bowl, combine first 6 ingredients. In another bowl, combine remaining ingredients. Stir into the dry ingredients just until moistened.
2. Pour into a greased 9x5-in. loaf pan. Bake until a toothpick comes out clean, 30-35 minutes. Cool 10 minutes before removing from pan to a wire rack. Serve warm. Refrigerate leftovers.
1 slice: 199 cal., 12g fat (7g sat. fat), 55mg chol., 338mg sod., 16g carb. (1g sugars, 1g fiber), 7g pro.

AUTUMN
APPLE TORTE

Low Country Boil

- Frogmore Stew
- Oven-Fried Cornbread
- Sweet Tea Boysenberry Shandy
- Favorite Chocolate-Bourbon Pecan Tart

FROGMORE STEW

OVEN-FRIED
CORNBREAD

FROGMORE STEW

This picnic-style medley of shrimp, smoked kielbasa, corn and spuds is a specialty of South Carolina cuisine. It's commonly dubbed Frogmore stew or Beaufort stew in recognition of both of the low country communities that lay claim to its origin. Whatever you call it, this one-pot wonder won't disappoint!
—Taste of Home *Test Kitchen*

PREP: 10 MIN. • **COOK:** 35 MIN.
MAKES: 8 SERVINGS

16 cups water
1 large sweet onion, quartered
3 Tbsp. seafood seasoning
2 medium lemons, halved, optional
1 lb. small red potatoes
1 lb. smoked kielbasa or fully cooked hot links, cut into 1-in. pieces
4 medium ears sweet corn, cut into thirds
2 lbs. uncooked medium shrimp, peeled and deveined
  Seafood cocktail sauce
  Melted butter
  Additional seafood seasoning

1. In a stockpot, combine water, onion, seafood seasoning and, if desired, lemons; bring to a boil. Add potatoes; cook, uncovered, 10 minutes. Add the kielbasa and corn; return to a boil. Reduce heat and simmer, uncovered, until potatoes are tender 10-12 minutes. Add shrimp; cook until shrimp turn pink, 2-3 minutes longer.
2. Drain; transfer to a bowl. Serve with cocktail sauce, butter and additional seafood seasoning.
1 serving: 369 cal., 18g fat (6g sat. fat), 175mg chol., 751mg sod., 24g carb. (7g sugars, 2g fiber), 28g pro.

OVEN-FRIED CORNBREAD

Nothing says good southern cooking like a crisp cornbread baked in a cast-iron skillet. This is an old family recipe that has been passed down to each generation.
—Emory Doty, Jasper, GA

PREP: 20 MIN. • **BAKE:** 15 MIN.
MAKES: 8 SERVINGS

4 Tbsp. canola oil, divided
1½ cups finely ground white cornmeal
¼ cup sugar
2 tsp. baking powder
1 tsp. baking soda
1 tsp. salt
2 large eggs, room temperature
2 cups buttermilk

1. Place 2 Tbsp. oil in a 10-in. cast-iron skillet; place in oven. Preheat oven to 450°. Whisk together the cornmeal, sugar, baking powder, baking soda and salt. In another bowl, whisk together eggs, buttermilk and remaining 2 Tbsp. oil. Add to the cornmeal mixture; stir just until moistened.
2. Carefully remove hot skillet from oven. Add batter; bake until golden brown and a toothpick inserted in center comes out clean, 15-20 minutes. Cut into wedges; serve warm.
1 wedge: 238 cal., 9g fat (1g sat. fat), 49mg chol., 709mg sod., 33g carb. (10g sugars, 1g fiber), 6g pro.

KITCHEN TIP: Jazz things up a bit by adding chopped green onion and/or small cubes of cooked ham to the batter.

SWEET TEA
BOYSENBERRY
SHANDY

FAVORITE CHOCOLATE-BOURBON PECAN TART

I grew up in Louisiana, where, as in most of the South, pecan pie is a staple during the holidays. When I tasted my first chocolate pecan pie, it blew my mind! I decided to boost the decadence of this dessert by adding bourbon, a great complement for the chocolate, to the pie, and by drizzling caramel on top.
—Amber Needham, San Antonio, TX

PREP: 15 MIN. • **BAKE:** 30 MIN. + COOLING
MAKES: 12 SERVINGS

Pastry for single-crust pie (9 in.)
- ½ cup semisweet chocolate chips
- 2 large eggs, room temperature
- ¾ cup dark corn syrup
- ½ cup sugar
- ¼ cup butter, melted
- 2 Tbsp. bourbon
- ¼ tsp. salt
- 1 cup pecan halves, toasted
- ¼ cup hot caramel ice cream topping

1. Preheat oven to 375°. On a lightly floured surface, roll dough to a 12-in. circle. Press onto bottom and up side of an ungreased 11-in. tart pan with removable bottom. Sprinkle with the chocolate chips.
2. Beat eggs, corn syrup, sugar, butter, bourbon and salt. Stir in pecans. Pour over chocolate chips. Bake until center is just set and crust is golden brown, 30-35 minutes.
3. Cool on a wire rack. Cut into slices. Serve with caramel topping.
NOTE: To toast nuts, bake in a shallow pan in a 350° oven for 5-10 minutes or cook in a skillet over low heat until lightly browned, stirring occasionally.
1 piece: 357 cal., 20g fat (9g sat. fat), 61mg chol., 250mg sod., 43g carb. (32g sugars, 2g fiber), 4g pro.

PASTRY FOR SINGLE-CRUST PIE (9 INCHES): Combine 1¼ cups all-purpose flour and ¼ tsp. salt; cut in ½ cup cold butter until crumbly. Gradually add 3-5 Tbsp. ice water, tossing with a fork until dough holds together when pressed. Cover and refrigerate 1 hour.

SWEET TEA BOYSENBERRY SHANDY

I love an ice-cold beer on a hot summer day. I also love sweet tea, so one day I got the great idea to mix the two. Wow! It was absolutely delish. I experimented with different flavorings, and this combo was my favorite.
—Kelly Williams, Forked River, NJ

PREP: 10 MIN. • **COOK:** 5 MIN. + CHILLING
MAKES: 12 SERVINGS (2¼ QT.)

- 1½ cups water
- 4 tea bags
- ¾ cup sugar
- ¾ cup boysenberry syrup
- 4 cups cold water
- 3 bottles (12 oz. each) beer or white ale, chilled
- 1 medium orange, sliced, optional

1. In a large saucepan, bring water to a boil; remove from heat. Add tea bags; steep, covered, 3-5 minutes, according to taste. Discard tea bags. Stir in sugar and syrup until dissolved. Stir in cold water. Transfer to a 3-qt. pitcher and refrigerate until cold.
2. Stir the beer into the tea mixture; serve immediately. If desired, top with orange slices.
¾ cup: 137 cal., 0 fat (0 sat. fat), 0 chol., 5mg sod., 29g carb. (26g sugars, 0 fiber), 0 pro.

FAVORITE
CHOCOLATE-BOURBON
PECAN TART

Spice Things Up

- Onion & Green Chile Enchiladas
- Eddie's Favorite Fiesta Corn
- Spicy Pork & Green Chili Verde
- Agua de Jamaica

ONION & GREEN CHILE ENCHILADAS

ONION & GREEN CHILE ENCHILADAS

When we have guests, they lobby for my famous enchiladas. I usually make a meatless version, but feel free to add cooked chicken.
—*Anthony Bolton, Bellevue, NE*

PREP: 20 MIN. • **BAKE:** 20 MIN.
MAKES: 6 SERVINGS

- 2 Tbsp. butter
- 3 large onions, sliced (about 6 cups)
- 2 cups shredded cheddar cheese, divided
- 1 cup sour cream
- ⅓ cup salsa
- 2 Tbsp. reduced-sodium taco seasoning
- 12 flour tortillas (6 in.)
- 2 cans (10 oz. each) green enchilada sauce
  Minced fresh cilantro, optional

1. Preheat oven to 350°. In a large skillet, heat butter over medium heat. Add the onions; cook and stir under tender and golden brown, 8-10 minutes. Cool the onions slightly.
2. Meanwhile, in a large bowl, combine 1 cup cheese, sour cream, salsa and taco seasoning. Stir in cooled onions.
3. Place 2 Tbsp. mixture off center on each tortilla. Roll up and place in a well-greased 13x9-in. baking dish, seam side down. Top with sauce; sprinkle with remaining 1 cup cheese.
4. Bake, uncovered, until heated through and cheese is melted, 20-25 minutes. Sprinkle with cilantro if desired.
2 enchiladas: 561 cal., 32g fat (18g sat. fat), 76mg chol., 1466mg sod., 50g carb. (9g sugars, 4g fiber), 17g pro.

EDDIE'S FAVORITE FIESTA CORN

EDDIE'S FAVORITE FIESTA CORN

When sweet corn is available, I love to make this splurge of a side dish. Frozen corn works, but taste as you go and add sugar if needed.
—*Anthony Bolton, Bellevue, NE*

PREP: 15 MIN. • **COOK:** 25 MIN.
MAKES: 8 SERVINGS

- ½ lb. bacon strips, chopped
- 5 cups fresh or frozen super sweet corn
- 1 medium sweet red pepper, finely chopped
- 1 medium sweet yellow pepper, finely chopped
- 1 pkg. (8 oz.) reduced-fat cream cheese
- ½ cup half-and-half cream
- 1 can (4 oz.) chopped green chiles, optional
- 2 tsp. sugar
- 1 tsp. pepper
- ¼ tsp. salt

1. In a 6-qt. stockpot, cook bacon over medium heat until crisp, stirring occasionally. Remove with a slotted spoon; drain on paper towels. Discard drippings, reserving 1 Tbsp. in pan.
2. Add corn, red pepper and yellow pepper to drippings; cook and stir over medium-high heat until tender, 5-6 minutes. Stir in the remaining ingredients until blended; bring to a boil. Reduce heat; simmer, covered, until thickened, 8-10 minutes.
⅔ cup: 249 cal., 14g fat (7g sat. fat), 39mg chol., 399mg sod., 22g carb. (9g sugars, 2g fiber), 10g pro.

SPICY PORK &
GREEN CHILI
VERDE

SPICY PORK &
GREEN CHILI VERDE

My pork chili is brimming with poblano
and sweet red peppers for a hearty kick.
Serve it with sour cream, Monterey Jack
and tortilla chips.
—*Anthony Bolton, Bellevue, NE*

PREP: 40 MIN. + STANDING
COOK: 25 MIN. • **MAKES:** 6 SERVINGS

- 6 poblano peppers
- 2 Tbsp. butter
- 1½ lbs. pork tenderloin, cut into
  1-in. pieces
- 2 medium sweet red or yellow
  peppers, coarsely chopped
- 1 large sweet onion, coarsely
  chopped
- 1 jalapeno pepper, seeded and finely
  chopped
- 2 Tbsp. chili powder
- 2 garlic cloves, minced
- 1 tsp. salt
- ¼ tsp. ground nutmeg
- 2 cups chicken broth
  Optional toppings: sour cream,
  shredded Monterey Jack cheese,
  crumbled tortilla chips and lime
  wedges

1. Place poblano peppers on a foil-lined
baking sheet. Broil 4 in. from heat until
skins blister, about 5 minutes. With
tongs, rotate peppers a quarter turn.
Broil and rotate until all sides are
blistered and blackened. Immediately
place peppers in a large bowl; let stand,
covered, 10 minutes.
2. Peel off and discard charred skin.
Remove and discard stems and seeds.
Finely chop peppers.
3. In a 6-qt. stockpot, heat butter over
medium heat. Brown pork in batches.
Remove with a slotted spoon.
4. To same pan, add the red peppers,
onion and jalapeno; cook, covered, over
medium heat until tender, 8-10 minutes,
stirring occasionally. Stir in chili powder,
garlic, salt and nutmeg. Add the broth,
roasted peppers and pork; bring to a
boil. Reduce heat; simmer, uncovered,
until pork is tender, 10-15 minutes. Serve
with toppings as desired.
1 cup: 235 cal., 9g fat (4g sat. fat), 75mg
chol., 913mg sod.,14g carb. (8g sugars,
4g fiber), 25g pro.

AGUA DE JAMAICA

This is an iced tea made from hibiscus.
It's tart and deep red like cranberry juice.
Add rum if you like.
—*Adan Franco, Milwaukee, WI*

PREP: 15 MIN. + CHILLING
MAKES: 6 SERVINGS

- 1 cup dried hibiscus flowers or
  6 hibiscus tea bags
- 5 cups water, divided
- 1½ tsp. grated lime zest
- ½ cup sugar
- 1 cup rum, optional
  Mint sprigs, optional

1. Rinse flowers in cold water. In a large
saucepan, combine 3 cups water,
flowers and lime zest. Bring to a boil.
Reduce the heat; simmer, uncovered,
10 minutes.
2. Remove from the heat; let stand
15 minutes. Strain mixture, discarding
flowers and zest; transfer to a large
bowl. Add sugar and remaining 2 cups
water, stirring until sugar is dissolved.
If desired, stir in rum. Refrigerate until
cold. Add mint sprigs if desired.
¾ cup: 67 cal., 0 fat (0 sat. fat), 0 chol., 2mg
sod.,17g carb. (17g sugars, 0 fiber), 0 pro.

AGUA DE JAMAICA

Classic Roast Beef Dinner

- Peppery Roast Beef
- Roasted Red Pepper Green Beans
- Raw Cauliflower Tabbouleh
- Biltmore's Bread Pudding

PEPPERY ROAST BEEF

PEPPERY ROAST BEEF

With its spicy coating and creamy horseradish sauce, this tender roast is sure to be the star of any meal, whether it's a sit-down dinner or serve-yourself potluck.
—*Maureen Brand, Somers, IA*

PREP: 15 MIN. • **BAKE:** 2½ HOURS + STANDING
MAKES: 12 SERVINGS

- 1 Tbsp. olive oil
- 1 Tbsp. seasoned pepper
- 2 garlic cloves, minced
- ½ tsp. dried thyme
- ¼ tsp. salt
- 1 boneless beef eye round or top round roast (4 to 5 lbs.)

HORSERADISH SAUCE
- 1 cup sour cream
- 2 Tbsp. lemon juice
- 2 Tbsp. milk
- 2 Tbsp. prepared horseradish
- 1 Tbsp. Dijon mustard
- ¼ tsp. salt
- ⅛ tsp. pepper

1. Preheat the oven to 325°. In a small bowl, combine the oil, seasoned pepper, garlic, thyme and salt; rub over roast. Place fat side up on a rack in a shallow roasting pan.
2. Bake, uncovered, 2½ to 3 hours or until meat reaches desired doneness (for medium-rare, a thermometer should read 135°; medium, 140°; medium-well, 145°). Let the roast stand 10 minutes before slicing.
3. In a small bowl, combine the sauce ingredients. Serve with roast.

4 oz. cooked beef with about 1 Tbsp. sauce: 228 cal., 10g fat (4g sat. fat), 83mg chol., 211mg sod., 3g carb. (1g sugars, 0 fiber), 30g pro.

ROASTED
RED PEPPER
GREEN BEANS

ROASTED RED PEPPER GREEN BEANS

This recipe showcases a creamy sauce with a tasty shallot-and-chive cheese. The toasted pine nuts add crunch. Just a few ingredients—so easy!
—*Becky Ellis, Roanoke, VA*

TAKES: 20 MIN. • **MAKES:** 10 SERVINGS

- 2 lbs. fresh green beans, trimmed
- 1 Tbsp. butter
- ½ cup pine nuts
  Dash salt
- 1 pkg. (5.2 oz.) shallot-chive spreadable cheese
- 1 jar (8 oz.) roasted sweet red peppers, drained and chopped

1. In a pot of boiling water, cook green beans until tender, 6-8 minutes.
2. Meanwhile, in a large skillet, melt the butter over medium heat. Add pine nuts; cook and stir until lightly browned, 3-4 minutes. Remove from heat; sprinkle with salt.
3. Drain beans; return to pot. Place cheese over warm beans to soften; toss to coat. Add red peppers; toss to combine. Sprinkle with pine nuts. Serve immediately.

¾ cup: 152 cal., 12g fat (5g sat. fat), 18mg chol., 341mg sod., 9g carb. (3g sugars, 3g fiber), 4g pro.

RAW CAULIFLOWER TABBOULEH

BILTMORE'S BREAD PUDDING

Here's one of our classic dessert recipes. A golden caramel sauce enhances the rich bread pudding.
—*Biltmore Estate, Asheville, NC*

PREP: 30 MIN. • **BAKE:** 40 MIN.
MAKES: 12 SERVINGS

8	cups cubed day-old bread
9	large eggs
2¼	cups 2% milk
1¾	cups heavy whipping cream
1	cup sugar
¾	cup butter, melted
3	tsp. vanilla extract
1½	tsp. ground cinnamon

CARAMEL SAUCE

1	cup sugar
¼	cup water
1	Tbsp. lemon juice
2	Tbsp. butter
1	cup heavy whipping cream

1. Place bread cubes in a greased 13x9-in. baking dish. In a large bowl, whisk the eggs, milk, cream, sugar, butter, vanilla and cinnamon. Pour evenly over bread.
2. Bake, uncovered, at 350° until a knife inserted in the center comes out clean, 40-45 minutes. Let stand for 5 minutes before cutting.
3. Meanwhile, in a small saucepan, bring sugar, water and lemon juice to a boil. Reduce heat to medium; cook until sugar is dissolved and mixture turns a golden amber color. Stir in butter until melted. Gradually stir in cream. Serve with the bread pudding.

1 piece: 581 cal., 39g fat (23g sat. fat), 273mg chol., 345mg sod., 49g carb. (37g sugars, 1g fiber), 9g pro.

KITCHEN TIP: For a fast, fruity twist, top individual servings with a sprinkling of berries, like blackberries or raspberries.

RAW CAULIFLOWER TABBOULEH

This recipe is super easy and fast to make. I love that I can offer it to my guests with special dietary restrictions.
—*Maiah Miller, Montclair, VA*

PREP: 10 MIN. + CHILLING • **MAKES:** 6 CUPS

1	medium head cauliflower
½	cup oil-packed sun-dried tomatoes
12	pitted Greek olives
2	cups fresh parsley leaves
1	cup fresh cilantro leaves
1	Tbsp. white wine vinegar or cider vinegar
¼	tsp. salt
¼	tsp. pepper

Core and coarsely chop cauliflower. In batches, pulse cauliflower in a food processor until it resembles rice (do not overprocess). Transfer to a large bowl. Add the remaining ingredients to food processor; pulse until finely chopped. Add to cauliflower; toss to combine. Refrigerate 1 hour before serving to allow flavors to blend.
¾ cup: 55 cal., 3g fat (0 sat. fat), 0 chol., 215mg sod., 7g carb. (2g sugars, 2g fiber), 2g pro.

BILTMORE'S
BREAD
PUDDING

Old-World Flavor

- Pork Shepherd's Pie
- Garlic-Herb Pattypan Squash
- Old-World Rye Bread
- Butternut Harvest Pies

PORK SHEPHERD'S PIE

PORK SHEPHERD'S PIE

Of all the shepherd's pie recipes I've tried through the years, this one is definitely the best. I enjoy cooking for my family, who all agree this meat pie is a keeper.
—*Mary Arthurs, Etobicoke, ON*

PREP: 30 MIN. • **BAKE:** 45 MIN.
MAKES: 6 SERVINGS

PORK LAYER
- 1   lb. ground pork
- 1   small onion, chopped
- 2   garlic cloves, minced
- 1   cup cooked rice
- ½   cup pork gravy or ¼ cup chicken broth
- ½   tsp. salt
- ½   tsp. dried thyme

CABBAGE LAYER
- 1   medium carrot, diced
- 1   small onion, chopped
- 2   Tbsp. butter or margarine
- 6   cups chopped cabbage
- 1   cup chicken broth
- ½   tsp. salt
- ¼   tsp. pepper

POTATO LAYER
- 2   cups mashed potatoes
- ¼   cup shredded cheddar cheese

In a skillet over medium heat, brown pork until no longer pink. Add onion and garlic. Cook until vegetables are tender; drain. Stir in rice, gravy, salt and thyme. Spoon into a greased 11x7-in. baking dish. In the same skillet, saute carrot and onion in butter over medium heat for 5 minutes. Stir in cabbage; cook for 1 minute. Add broth, salt and pepper; cover and cook for 10 minutes. Spoon over pork layer. Spoon or pipe mashed potatoes on top; sprinkle with cheese. Bake, uncovered, at 350° until browned, about 45 minutes.

1 cup: 365 cal., 19g fat (8g sat. fat), 66mg chol., 1045mg sod., 28g carb. (5g sugars, 4g fiber), 19g pro.

GARLIC-HERB PATTYPAN SQUASH

The first time I grew a garden, I harvested summer squash and cooked it with garlic and herbs. Using pattypan squash works beautifully, too.
—*Kaycee Mason, Siloam Spgs, AR*

TAKES: 25 MIN. • **MAKES:** 4 SERVINGS

- 5   cups halved small pattypan squash (about 1¼ lbs.)
- 1   Tbsp. olive oil
- 2   garlic cloves, minced
- ½   tsp. salt
- ¼   tsp. dried oregano
- ¼   tsp. dried thyme
- ¼   tsp. pepper
- 1   Tbsp. minced fresh parsley

Preheat oven to 425°. Place squash in a greased 15x10x1-in. baking pan. Mix oil, garlic, salt, oregano, thyme and pepper; drizzle over squash. Toss to coat. Roast until tender, 15-20 minutes, stirring occasionally. Sprinkle with parsley.

⅔ cup: 58 cal., 3g fat (0 sat. fat), 0 chol., 296mg sod., 6g carb. (3g sugars, 2g fiber), 2g pro. **Diabetic exchanges:** 1 vegetable, ½ fat.

OLD-WORLD RYE BREAD

BUTTERNUT HARVEST PIES

This egg- and dairy-free pie is a great alternative to standard pumpkin pie! We love to make the pies with squash from our garden. Feel free to spice up this pie even more, adding your favorite spices. You'll be glad the recipe makes two pies.
—*Juliana Thetford, Ellwood City, PA*

PREP: 65 MIN.
BAKE: 40 MIN. + CHILLING
MAKES: 2 PIES (6 SERVINGS EACH)

- 1 large butternut squash (about 4 lbs.)
- 1 pkg. (10½ oz.) silken firm tofu
- 1 cup sugar
- ⅓ cup cornstarch
- 2 Tbsp. honey
- 2 tsp. ground cinnamon
- 1 tsp. ground ginger
- 1 tsp. ground nutmeg or ground mace
- 2 graham cracker crusts (9 in.) Sweetened whipped cream, optional

1. Preheat oven to 400°. Halve squash lengthwise; discard seeds. Place squash on a baking sheet, cut side down. Roast until tender, 45-55 minutes. Cool slightly. Scoop out pulp and mash (you should have about 4 cups).
2. Place tofu, sugar, cornstarch, honey and spices in a food processor; process until smooth. Add squash; pulse just until blended. Divide between crusts.
3. Bake at 400° until a knife inserted in center comes out clean, 40-50 minutes. Cool 1 hour on a wire rack. Refrigerate, covered, until cold. If desired, serve with whipped cream.
1 piece: 281 cal., 8g fat (2g sat. fat), 0 chol., 174mg sod., 51g carb. (35g sugars, 3g fiber), 4g pro.

OLD-WORLD RYE BREAD

Rye and caraway lend flavor to this bread, while the surprise ingredient of baking cocoa gives it a rich, dark color. I sometimes stir in a cup each of raisins and walnuts.
—*Perlene Hoekema, Lynden, WA*

PREP: 25 MIN. + RISING
BAKE: 35 MIN. + COOLING
MAKES: 2 LOAVES (12 PIECES EACH)

- 2 pkg. (¼ oz. each) active dry yeast
- 1½ cups warm water (110° to 115°)
- ½ cup molasses
- 6 Tbsp. butter, softened
- 2 cups rye flour
- ¼ cup baking cocoa
- 2 Tbsp. caraway seeds
- 2 tsp. salt
- 3½ to 4 cups all-purpose flour
  Cornmeal

1. In a large bowl, dissolve yeast in warm water. Beat in the molasses, butter, rye flour, cocoa, caraway seeds, salt and 2 cups all-purpose flour until smooth. Stir in enough remaining all-purpose flour to form a stiff dough.
2. Turn onto a floured surface; knead until smooth and elastic, 6-8 minutes. Place in a greased bowl, turning once to grease top. Cover and let rise in a warm place until doubled, about 1½ hours.
3. Punch dough down. Turn onto a lightly floured surface; divide in half. Shape each piece into a loaf about 10 in. long. Grease 2 baking sheets and sprinkle with cornmeal. Place loaves on prepared pans. Cover and let rise until doubled, about 1 hour.
4. Bake at 350° until bread sounds hollow when tapped, 35-40 minutes. Remove from pans to wire racks to cool.
1 piece: 146 cal., 3g fat (2g sat. fat), 8mg chol., 229mg sod., 26g carb. (5g sugars, 2g fiber), 3g pro.

BUTTERNUT
HARVEST PIES

Taste of Italy

- Sausage Lasagna
- Risotto Balls (Arancini)
- Italian Pinwheel Rolls
- Italian Cream Cheese Cake

SAUSAGE LASAGNA

The idea for this sausage lasagna recipe comes from my mother-in-law, who always makes it for my three boys on special holidays. I've put an easy twist on Carole's classic dish, and it's become one of my go-to dinners as well!

—*Blair Lonergan, Rochelle, VA*

PREP: 45 MIN. • **BAKE:** 35 MIN. + STANDING
MAKES: 12 SERVINGS

- 1 **lb. bulk Italian sausage**
- 1 **medium onion, chopped**
- 2 **garlic cloves, minced**
- 1 **can (6 oz.) tomato paste**
- 1 **can (28 oz.) crushed tomatoes**
- 1 **can (8 oz.) tomato sauce**
- 3 **tsp. dried basil**
- ¾ **tsp. pepper, divided**
- ¼ **tsp. salt**
- 1 **large egg, lightly beaten**
- 1 **carton (15 oz.) whole-milk ricotta cheese**
- 1½ **cups grated Parmesan cheese, divided**
- 12 **no-cook lasagna noodles**
- 4 **cups shredded part-skim mozzarella cheese**

1. Preheat oven to 400°. In a large skillet, cook and crumble sausage with onion over medium heat until no longer pink, 5-7 minutes; drain. Add garlic and tomato paste; cook and stir 1 minute.
2. Stir in tomatoes, tomato sauce, basil, ½ tsp. pepper and salt; bring to a boil. Reduce heat; simmer, uncovered, until slightly thickened, 10-15 minutes.
3. In a bowl, mix egg, ricotta cheese, 1¼ cups Parmesan cheese and the remaining ¼ tsp. pepper. Spread 1½ cups meat sauce into a greased 13x9-in. baking dish. Add a layer of 4 noodles, 1½ cups ricotta cheese mixture, 1½ cups mozzarella cheese and 1½ cups sauce. Repeat layers. Top with the remaining noodles, sauce and mozzarella and Parmesan cheeses.
4. Cover with greased foil; baked for 30 minutes. Uncover and bake until lightly browned and heated through, 5-10 minutes. Let stand 15 minutes before serving.
1 piece: 416 cal., 23g fat (11g sat. fat), 83mg chol., 978mg sod., 29g carb. (8g sugars, 3g fiber), 25g pro.

RISOTTO BALLS (ARANCINI)

RISOTTO BALLS (ARANCINI)

My Italian grandma made these for me. I still ask for them when I visit her, and so do my children. They freeze really well, so when I know I'm going to be busy I make them ahead of time.

—*Gretchen Whelan, San Francisco, CA*

PREP: 35 MIN. • **BAKE:** 25 MIN. • **MAKES:** ABOUT 3 DOZEN

- 1½ **cups water**
- 1 **cup uncooked arborio rice**
- 1 **tsp. salt**
- 2 **large eggs, lightly beaten**
- ⅔ **cup sun-dried tomato pesto**
- 2 **cups panko bread crumbs, divided**
  Marinara sauce, warmed

1. Preheat the oven to 375°. In a large saucepan, combine water, arborio rice and salt; bring to a boil. Reduce heat; simmer, covered, until liquid is absorbed and rice is tender, 18-20 minutes. Let stand, covered, 10 minutes. Transfer to a large bowl; cool slightly. Add eggs and pesto; stir in 1 cup bread crumbs.
2. Place the remaining bread crumbs in a shallow bowl. Shape rice mixture into 1¼-in. balls. Roll in bread crumbs, patting to help coating adhere. Place on greased 15x10x1-in. baking pans. Bake until golden brown, 25-30 minutes. Serve with marinara sauce.
1 appetizer: 42 cal., 1g fat (0 sat. fat), 10mg chol., 125mg sod., 7g carb. (1g sugars, 0 fiber), 1g pro. **Diabetic exchanges:** ½ starch.

ITALIAN PINWHEEL ROLLS

ITALIAN CREAM CHEESE CAKE

Buttermilk makes every bite of this awesome Italian cream cheese cake recipe moist and flavorful. I rely on this recipe year-round.
—*Joyce Lutz, Centerview, MO*

PREP: 40 MIN. • **BAKE:** 20 MIN. + COOLING
MAKES: 16 SERVINGS

- ½ cup butter, softened
- ½ cup shortening
- 2 cups sugar
- 5 large eggs, separated
- 1 tsp. vanilla extract
- 2 cups all-purpose flour
- 1 tsp. baking soda
- 1 cup buttermilk
- 1½ cups sweetened shredded coconut
- 1 cup chopped pecans

CREAM CHEESE FROSTING
- 11 oz. cream cheese, softened
- ¾ cup butter, softened
- 6 cups confectioners' sugar
- 1½ tsp. vanilla extract
- ¾ cup chopped pecans

1. Preheat oven to 350°. Grease and flour three 9-in. round baking pans. In a large bowl, cream the butter, shortening and granulated sugar until light and fluffy, 5-7 minutes. Beat in the egg yolks and vanilla. Combine flour and baking soda; add to creamed mixture alternately with the buttermilk. Beat until just combined. Stir in coconut and pecans.
2. In another bowl, beat egg whites with clean beaters until stiff but not dry. Fold one-fourth of the egg whites into batter, then fold in remaining whites. Pour into prepared pans.
3. Bake until a toothpick inserted in the center comes out clean, 20-25 minutes. Cool 10 minutes before removing from pans to wire racks to cool completely.
4. For frosting, beat the cream cheese and butter until smooth. Beat in the confectioners' sugar and vanilla until fluffy. Stir in pecans. Spread frosting between layers and over top and side of cake. Refrigerate.
1 piece: 736 cal., 41g fat (19g sat. fat), 117mg chol., 330mg sod., 90g carb. (75g sugars, 2g fiber), 7g pro.

ITALIAN PINWHEEL ROLLS

Parmesan cheese, garlic and oregano make these rolls hard to resist. My family gets hungry when they smell them baking.
—*Patricia FitzGerald, Candor, NY*

PREP: 35 MIN. + RISING • **BAKE:** 25 MIN.
MAKES: 1 DOZEN

- 1 pkg. (¼ oz.) active dry yeast
- 1 cup warm water (110° to 115°)
- 1½ tsp. sugar
- 1½ tsp. butter, softened
- 1 tsp. salt
- 2¼ to 2½ cups bread flour

FILLING
- 2 Tbsp. butter, melted
- ¼ cup grated Parmesan cheese
- 2 Tbsp. minced fresh parsley
- 6 garlic cloves, minced
- 1 tsp. dried oregano

1. In a bowl, dissolve yeast in warm water. Add the sugar, butter, salt and 1 cup flour; beat until smooth. Stir in enough of the remaining flour to form a soft dough.
2. Turn onto a floured surface; knead dough until it's smooth and elastic, 6-8 minutes. Place in a bowl coated with cooking spray, turning once to coat top. Cover and let rise in a warm place until doubled, about 1 hour.
3. Punch dough down. Turn onto a lightly floured surface. Roll into a 12x10-in. rectangle. Brush with the melted butter; sprinkle the cheese, parsley, garlic and oregano to within ½ in. of edges. Roll up jelly-roll style, starting with a long side; pinch seam to seal. Cut into 12 rolls.
4. Place rolls cut side up in a 13x9-in. baking pan coated with cooking spray. Cover and let rise until doubled, about 30 minutes.
5. Bake at 350° until golden brown, 25-30 minutes. Remove from pan to a wire rack.
1 roll: 110 cal., 3g fat (2g sat. fat), 8mg chol., 253mg sod., 18g carb. (1g sugars, 1g fiber), 4g pro. **Diabetic exchanges:** 1 starch, ½ fat.

ITALIAN
CREAM CHEESE CAKE

Easy Fish Menu

- Tuscan Fish Packets
- Green Salad with Berries
- Cheese & Garlic Biscuits
- Carrot Blueberry Cupcakes

TUSCAN FISH PACKETS

My husband does a lot of fishing, so I'm always looking for different ways to serve his catches. A professional chef was kind enough to share this recipe with me, and I played around with some different veggie combinations until I found the one that my family liked best.

—Kathy Morrow, Hubbard, OH

TAKES: 30 MIN. • **MAKES:** 4 SERVINGS

- 1 can (15 oz.) great northern beans, rinsed and drained
- 4 plum tomatoes, chopped
- 1 small zucchini, chopped
- 1 medium onion, chopped
- 1 garlic clove, minced
- ¼ cup white wine
- ¾ tsp. salt, divided
- ¼ tsp. pepper, divided
- 4 tilapia fillets (6 oz. each)
- 1 medium lemon, cut into 8 thin slices

1. Preheat oven to 400°. In a bowl, combine beans, tomatoes, zucchini, onion, garlic, wine, ½ tsp. salt and ⅛ tsp. pepper.
2. Rinse fish and pat dry. Place each fillet on an 18x12-in. piece of heavy-duty foil; season with remaining ¼ tsp. salt and ⅛ tsp. pepper. Spoon bean mixture over fish; top with lemon slices. Fold foil around fish and crimp edges to seal. Transfer packets to a baking sheet.
3. Bake until fish just begins to flake easily with a fork and vegetables are tender, 15-20 minutes. Be careful of escaping steam when opening packets.
1 serving: 270 cal., 2g fat (1g sat. fat), 83mg chol., 658mg sod., 23g carb. (4g sugars, 7g fiber), 38g pro. **Diabetic exchanges:** 5 lean meat, 1 starch, 1 vegetable.

GREEN SALAD WITH BERRIES

GREEN SALAD WITH BERRIES

For a snappy salad that draws a crowd, I do a wonderful combo of spinach, berries and onion-y things. Raise your fork for this one.

—Aysha Schurman, Ammon, ID

TAKES: 15 MIN. • **MAKES:** 4 SERVINGS

- 1 cup torn romaine
- 1 cup fresh baby spinach
- 1 cup sliced fresh strawberries
- ½ cup thinly sliced celery
- ½ small red onion, thinly sliced
- ½ cup coarsely chopped walnuts
- 2 green onions, chopped
- ¼ cup raspberry vinaigrette
- 1 cup fresh raspberries

In a large bowl, combine the first 7 ingredients. To serve, drizzle with vinaigrette and toss to combine. Top with raspberries.
1 serving: 157 cal., 10g fat (1g sat. fat), 0 chol., 50mg sod., 15g carb. (8g sugars, 5g fiber), 4g pro. **Diabetic exchanges:** 2 fat, 1 vegetable, ½ fruit.

CHEESE & GARLIC BISCUITS

CARROT BLUEBERRY CUPCAKES

Carrots, blueberries, pineapple and zucchini make a unique and delicious combination in these little treats.
—*Patricia Kile, Elizabethtown, PA*

PREP: 35 MIN. • BAKE: 20 MIN. + COOLING
MAKES: 16 CUPCAKES

- 1 cup sugar
- ½ cup canola oil
- 2 large eggs, room temperature
- 1 tsp. vanilla extract
- 1½ cups all-purpose flour
- 1 tsp. baking powder
- 1 tsp. ground cinnamon
- ½ tsp. baking soda
- ½ tsp. salt
- 1 cup finely shredded carrots
- ¾ cup grated zucchini
- ½ cup unsweetened crushed pineapple, drained
- 1 cup fresh or frozen unsweetened blueberries

FROSTING
- 3 oz. cream cheese, softened
- ¼ cup butter, softened
- 2½ cups confectioners' sugar
- 1 tsp. vanilla extract
- ½ cup chopped pecans, optional
  Fresh blueberries, optional

1. In a small bowl, beat the sugar, oil, eggs and vanilla. In another large bowl, combine flour, baking powder, cinnamon, baking soda and salt; gradually beat into sugar mixture until blended. Stir in the carrots, zucchini and pineapple. Fold in blueberries.
2. Fill paper-lined muffin cups two-thirds full. Bake at 375° until a toothpick inserted in the center comes out clean, 18-22 minutes. Cool for 10 minutes before removing from pans to wire racks to cool completely.
3. For frosting, in a large bowl, beat cream cheese and butter until fluffy. Add confectioners' sugar and vanilla; beat until smooth. Frost cupcakes. If desired, top with pecans and fresh blueberries. Refrigerate leftovers.
1 cupcake: 294 cal., 13g fat (4g sat. fat), 40mg chol., 189mg sod., 44g carb. (33g sugars, 1g fiber), 3g pro.

CHEESE & GARLIC BISCUITS

My biscuits won the prize for best quick bread at my county fair. One of the judges liked them so much, she asked for the recipe! These buttery, savory biscuits go with just about anything.
—*Gloria Jarrett, Loveland, OH*

TAKES: 20 MIN. • MAKES: 2½ DOZEN

- 2½ cups biscuit/baking mix
- ¾ cup shredded sharp cheddar cheese
- 1 tsp. garlic powder
- 1 tsp. ranch salad dressing mix
- 1 cup buttermilk

TOPPING
- ½ cup butter, melted
- 1 Tbsp. minced chives
- ½ tsp. garlic powder
- ½ tsp. ranch salad dressing mix
- ¼ tsp. pepper

1. In a large bowl, combine the baking mix, cheese, garlic powder and salad dressing mix. Stir in the buttermilk just until moistened. Drop by tablespoonfuls onto greased baking sheets.
2. Bake at 450° until golden brown, 6-8 minutes. Meanwhile, combine the topping ingredients. Brush over biscuits. Serve warm.
1 biscuit: 81 cal., 5g fat (3g sat. fat), 11mg chol., 176mg sod., 7g carb. (1g sugars, 0 fiber), 2g pro.

CARROT
BLUEBERRY
CUPCAKES

CHAPTER 2

ONE-DISH SUNDAY DINNERS

When it comes to comfort and convenience, few recipes
can top a meal-in-one specialty. Get cozy any time of year
with these hearty dishes that are guaranteed to satisfy.

SLOW-COOKED PORK STEW

Try this comforting stew that's easy to put together, but tastes like you've been working hard in the kitchen all day. It's even better served over polenta, egg noodles or mashed potatoes.
—*Nancy Elliott, Houston, TX*

PREP: 15 MIN. • **COOK:** 5 HOURS
MAKES: 8 SERVINGS

- 2 pork tenderloins (1 lb. each), cut into 2-in. pieces
- 1 tsp. salt
- ½ tsp. pepper
- 2 large carrots, cut into ½-in. slices
- 2 celery ribs, coarsely chopped
- 1 medium onion, coarsely chopped
- 3 cups beef broth
- 2 Tbsp. tomato paste
- ⅓ cup pitted dried plums (prunes), chopped
- 4 garlic cloves, minced
- 2 bay leaves
- 1 fresh rosemary sprig
- 1 fresh thyme sprig
- ⅓ cup Greek olives, optional
      Chopped fresh parsley, optional
      Hot cooked mashed potatoes, optional

1. Sprinkle pork with salt and pepper; transfer to a 4-qt. slow cooker. Add the carrots, celery and onion. In a small bowl, whisk the broth and tomato paste; pour over vegetables. Add plums, garlic, bay leaves, rosemary, thyme and, if desired, olives. Cook, covered, on low until meat and vegetables are tender, 5-6 hours.
2. Discard bay leaves, rosemary and thyme. If desired, sprinkle stew with parsley and serve with potatoes.

1 cup: 177 cal., 4g fat (1g sat. fat), 64mg chol., 698mg sod., 9g carb. (4g sugars, 1g fiber), 24g pro. **Diabetic exchanges:** 3 lean meat, ½ starch.

SERVE WITH:
Herb Quick Bread,
Page 82

CHICKEN MARSALA
LASAGNA

CHICKEN MARSALA LASAGNA

I love chicken Marsala, but most recipes don't yield enough to serve a crowd. This lasagna version can feed up to 12 people.
—*Debbie Shannon, Ringgold, GA*

PREP: 50 MIN. • **BAKE:** 50 MIN. + STANDING
MAKES: 12 SERVINGS

- 12 lasagna noodles
- 4 tsp. Italian seasoning, divided
- 1 tsp. salt
- ¾ lb. boneless skinless chicken breasts, cubed
- 1 Tbsp. olive oil
- ¼ cup finely chopped onion
- ½ cup butter, cubed
- ½ lb. sliced baby portobello mushrooms
- 12 garlic cloves, minced
- 1½ cups beef broth
- ¾ cup Marsala wine, divided
- ¼ tsp. coarsely ground pepper
- 3 Tbsp. cornstarch
- ½ cup finely chopped fully cooked ham
- 1 carton (15 oz.) ricotta cheese
- 1 pkg. (10 oz.) frozen chopped spinach, thawed and squeezed dry
- 2 cups shredded Italian cheese blend
- 1 cup grated Parmesan cheese, divided
- 2 large eggs, lightly beaten

1. Cook noodles according to package directions; drain. Meanwhile, mix 2 tsp. Italian seasoning and salt; sprinkle over chicken breasts. In a large skillet, heat oil over medium-high heat. Add chicken; saute until no longer pink. Remove and keep warm.

2. In same skillet, cook onion in butter over medium heat 2 minutes. Stir in the mushrooms; cook until tender, 4-5 minutes longer. Add garlic; cook and stir 2 minutes.
3. Stir in broth, ½ cup wine and pepper; bring to a boil. Mix the cornstarch and remaining ¼ cup wine until smooth; stir into pan. Bring to a boil; cook and stir until thickened, about 2 minutes. Stir in ham and chicken.
4. Preheat oven to 350°. Combine the ricotta cheese, spinach, Italian cheese blend, ¾ cup Parmesan cheese, eggs and remaining 2 tsp. Italian seasoning. Spread 1 cup chicken mixture onto the bottom of a greased 13x9-in. baking dish. Layer with 3 noodles, about ¾ cup chicken mixture and about 1 cup ricotta mixture. Repeat layers 3 times.
5. Bake lasagna, covered, 40 minutes. Sprinkle with the remaining ¼ cup Parmesan cheese. Bake, uncovered, until casserole is bubbly and cheese is melted, 10-15 minutes. Let stand for 10 minutes before cutting.
FREEZE OPTION: Cool unbaked lasagna; cover and freeze. To use, partially thaw in refrigerator overnight. Remove from refrigerator 30 minutes before baking. Preheat oven to 350°. Cover lasagna with foil; bake as directed until heated through and a thermometer inserted into the center reads 165°, increasing time to 45-50 minutes. Sprinkle with remaining Parmesan cheese. Bake, uncovered, until bubbly and cheese is melted, 10-15 minutes. Let stand 10 minutes before cutting.

1 piece: 388 cal., 20 g fat (12 g sat. fat), 107 mg chol., 749 mg sod., 27 g carb., 2 g fiber, 24 g pro.

RAVIOLI WITH CREAMY SQUASH SAUCE

Store-bought ravioli speeds assembly of this no-fuss recipe. It tastes so good, no one will notice that it's meatless.
—Taste of Home *Test Kitchen*

TAKES: 20 MIN. • **MAKES:** 4 SERVINGS

- 1 pkg. (9 oz.) refrigerated cheese ravioli
- 3 garlic cloves, minced
- 2 Tbsp. butter
- 1 pkg. (10 oz.) frozen cooked winter squash, thawed
- 1 pkg. (6 oz.) fresh baby spinach
- 1 cup heavy whipping cream
- ⅓ cup vegetable broth
- ¼ tsp. salt
- 1 cup chopped walnuts, toasted

1. Cook ravioli according to the package directions. Meanwhile, in a Dutch oven, saute garlic in butter for 1 minute. Add squash and spinach; cook until spinach is wilted, 2-3 minutes longer. Stir in the cream, broth and salt. Bring to a gentle boil; cook until slightly thickened, 6-8 minutes.
2. Drain ravioli; add to squash mixture. Toss to coat. Sprinkle with walnuts.
1¼ cups: 671 cal., 51g fat (22g sat. fat), 122mg chol., 578mg sod., 42g carb. (2g sugars, 7g fiber), 18g pro.

TILAPIA WITH CORN SALSA

My family loves fish, so this quick-cooking tilapia is popular at our house. Though it tastes as if it takes a long time, it cooks in minutes under the broiler. We enjoy it garnished with lemon wedges and served with couscous on the side.
—Brenda Coffey, Singer Island, FL

TAKES: 10 MIN. • **MAKES:** 4 SERVINGS

- 4 tilapia fillets (6 oz. each)
- 1 Tbsp. olive oil
- ¼ tsp. salt
- ¼ tsp. pepper
- 1 can (15 oz.) black beans, rinsed and drained
- 1 can (11 oz.) whole kernel corn, drained
- ½ cup Italian salad dressing
- 2 Tbsp. chopped green onion
- 2 Tbsp. chopped sweet red pepper

1. Drizzle both sides of fillets with oil; sprinkle with salt and pepper.
2. Broil 4-6 in. from the heat until fish flakes easily with a fork, 5-7 minutes. Meanwhile, in a small bowl, combine the remaining ingredients. Serve with fish.
1 fillet with ¾ cup salsa: 354 cal., 10g fat (2g sat. fat), 83mg chol., 934mg sod., 25g carb. (7g sugars, 6g fiber), 38g pro.

BEEF & BACON GNOCCHI SKILLET

This gnocchi dish tastes like a classic bacon cheeseburger. Top it as you would a burger—with ketchup, mustard, pickles or your favorite condiments.
—Ashley Lecker, Green Bay, WI

TAKES: 30 MIN. • **MAKES:** 6 SERVINGS

- 1 pkg. (16 oz.) potato gnocchi
- 1¼ lbs. lean ground beef (90% lean)
- 1 medium onion, chopped
- 8 cooked bacon strips, crumbled and divided
- 1 cup water
- ½ cup heavy whipping cream
- 1 Tbsp. ketchup
- ¼ tsp. salt
- ¼ tsp. pepper
- 1½ cups shredded cheddar cheese
- ½ cup chopped tomatoes
- 2 green onions, sliced

1. Preheat broiler. Cook the gnocchi according to package directions; drain.
2. Meanwhile, in a large cast-iron or other ovenproof skillet, cook beef and onion over medium heat until beef is no longer pink, 4-6 minutes, breaking meat into crumbles. Drain.
3. Stir in half the bacon; add gnocchi, water, cream and ketchup. Bring to a boil. Cook, stirring, over medium heat until sauce has thickened, 3-4 minutes. Add salt and pepper. Sprinkle with the cheddar cheese.
4. Broil 3-4 in. from heat until cheese has melted, 1-2 minutes. Top with tomatoes, green onions and remaining bacon.
1 cup: 573 cal., 31g fat (16g sat. fat), 136mg chol., 961mg sod., 35g carb. (7g sugars, 2g fiber), 36g pro.

SAUSAGE & SQUASH PENNE

I love using frozen cooked winter squash because the hard work—peeling, chopping and cooking—is all done for me.
—*Jennifer Roberts, South Burlington, VT*

TAKES: 30 MIN. • **MAKES:** 4 SERVINGS

- 2 cups uncooked penne pasta
- 1 pkg. (12 oz.) frozen cooked winter squash
- 2 Tbsp. olive oil
- 3 cooked Italian sausage links (4 oz. each), sliced
- 1 medium onion, chopped
- ¼ cup grated Parmesan cheese
- ¼ tsp. salt
- ¼ tsp. dried parsley flakes
- ¼ tsp. pepper
  Optional: Additional grated Parmesan cheese and minced fresh parsley

1. Cook pasta and squash according to package directions. Meanwhile, in a large skillet, heat oil over medium heat. Add sausage and onion; cook and stir until sausage is browned and onion is tender; keep warm.
2. In a small bowl, mix the cooked squash, cheese, salt, parsley and pepper until blended. Drain pasta; transfer to a serving plate. Spoon squash mixture over pasta; top with sausage mixture. If desired, sprinkle with additional cheese and parsley.
¾ cup pasta with ½ cup sausage and ¼ cup squash: 468 cal., 26g fat (8g sat. fat), 40mg chol., 705mg sod., 41g carb. (4g sugars, 4g fiber), 19g pro.

TAMALE PIE

The amount of spice in this recipe is just right for my family, who prefers things on the mild side. Make it once with these measurements, then spice it up a little more if you like!
—*Ruth Aden, Polson, MT*

PREP: 35 MIN. • **BAKE:** 30 MIN.
MAKES: 8 SERVINGS

- 1½ lbs. ground beef
- 2 cans (14½ oz. each) stewed tomatoes
- 1 medium onion, chopped
- ½ tsp. garlic powder
- ½ tsp. chili powder
- ¼ tsp. salt
- ¼ tsp. pepper
- 10 flour tortillas (6 in.)
- 3 cups (12 oz. each) shredded cheddar-Monterey Jack cheese or Colby-Jack cheese
- 1 can (2¼ oz.) sliced ripe olives, drained

1. In a skillet, brown ground beef; drain. Add tomatoes, onion and seasonings. Simmer, uncovered, for 20 minutes.
2. Arrange 5 tortillas in the bottom of a 13x9-in. baking dish, tearing tortillas as needed. Cover with half of the meat mixture, then half of the cheese. Repeat layers, using remaining tortillas, meat mixture and cheese. Sprinkle with olives.
3. Bake at 350° until heated through, about 30 minutes. Let stand a few minutes before serving.
1 piece: 428 cal., 24g fat (13g sat. fat), 79mg chol., 829mg sod., 24g carb. (4g sugars, 1g fiber), 29g pro.

GLAZED SMOKED CHOPS WITH PEARS

My husband would eat pork chops every day if he could. Luckily, they're good all sorts of ways, including with pears.
—*Lynn Moretti, Oconomowoc, WI*

TAKES: 30 MIN. • **MAKES:** 4 SERVINGS

- 4 smoked boneless pork chops
- 1 Tbsp. olive oil
- 1 large sweet onion, cut into thin wedges
- ½ cup dry red wine or reduced-sodium chicken broth
- 2 Tbsp. balsamic vinegar
- 2 Tbsp. honey
- 2 large ripe pears, cut into 1-in. wedges

1. Preheat oven to 350°. In an ovenproof skillet over medium-high heat, brown the pork chops on both sides; remove from pan.
2. In same pan, heat oil over medium heat; saute the onion until tender, 3-5 minutes. Add wine, vinegar and honey; bring to a boil, stirring to loosen the browned bits from pan. Reduce the heat; simmer, uncovered, until slightly thickened, about 5 minutes, stirring occasionally.
3. Return chops to pan; top with pears. Transfer to oven; bake until pears are tender, 10-15 minutes.
1 serving: 313 cal., 4g fat (6g sat. fat), 41mg chol., 1056mg sod., 34g carb. (26g sugars, 4g fiber), 22g pro.

PUFF PASTRY
CHICKEN POTPIE

PUFF PASTRY CHICKEN POTPIE

When my wife is craving comfort food, I whip up my chicken potpie. It's easy to make, sticks to your ribs and delivers soul-satisfying flavor.
—Nick Iverson, Denver, CO

PREP: 45 MIN. • **BAKE:** 45 MIN. + STANDING
MAKES: 8 SERVINGS

- 1 pkg. (17.3 oz.) frozen puff pastry, thawed
- 2 lbs. boneless skinless chicken breasts, cut into 1-in. pieces
- 1 tsp. salt, divided
- 1 tsp. pepper, divided
- 4 Tbsp. butter, divided
- 1 large onion, chopped
- 2 garlic cloves, minced
- 1 tsp. minced fresh thyme or ¼ tsp. dried thyme
- 1 tsp. minced fresh sage or ¼ tsp. rubbed sage
- ½ cup all-purpose flour
- 1½ cups chicken broth
- 1 cup plus 1 Tbsp. half-and-half cream, divided
- 2 cups frozen mixed vegetables (about 10 oz.)
- 1 Tbsp. lemon juice
- 1 large egg yolk

1. Preheat oven to 400°. On a lightly floured surface, roll each pastry sheet into a 12x10-in. rectangle. Cut 1 sheet crosswise into six 2-in. strips; cut the remaining sheet lengthwise into five 2-in. strips. On a baking sheet, closely weave strips to make a 12x10-in. lattice. Freeze while making filling.
2. Toss chicken with ½ tsp. each salt and pepper. In a large skillet, heat 1 Tbsp. butter over medium-high heat; saute chicken until browned, 5-7 minutes. Remove from pan.
3. In same skillet, heat remaining butter over medium-high heat; saute onion until tender, 5-7 minutes. Stir in garlic and herbs; cook 1 minute. Stir in the flour until blended; cook and stir 1 minute. Gradually stir in broth and 1 cup cream. Bring to a boil, stirring constantly; cook and stir until thickened, about 2 minutes.
4. Stir in vegetables, lemon juice, chicken and remaining ½ tsp. salt and pepper; return to a boil. Transfer to a greased 2½-qt. oblong baking dish. Top with the lattice, trimming to fit.
5. Whisk together the egg yolk and remaining cream; brush over pastry. Bake, uncovered, until bubbly and golden brown, 45-55 minutes. Cover loosely with foil if it starts getting too dark. Let stand 15 minutes before serving.
1 serving: 523 cal., 25g fat (10g sat. fat), 118mg chol., 768mg sod., 42g carb. (4g sugars, 6g fiber), 30g pro.

KITCHEN TIP: For a crispier upper crust, bake it separately on a rimmed baking sheet. Start by trimming the puff pastry lattice to fit your baking dish, then place it on a parchment-lined baking sheet. Bake at 400° for 20-25 minutes. Place crust on top of your hot filling before serving.

SLICED HAM WITH ROASTED VEGETABLES

To prepare this colorful, zesty oven meal, I shop in my backyard for the fresh garden vegetables and oranges (we have our own tree!) that spark the ham's hearty flavor. It's my family's favorite main dish.
—Margaret Pache, Mesa, AZ

PREP: 10 MIN. • **BAKE:** 35 MIN.
MAKES: 6 SERVINGS

- Cooking spray
- 6 medium potatoes, peeled and cubed
- 5 medium carrots, sliced
- 1 medium turnip, peeled and cubed
- 1 large onion, cut into thin wedges
- 6 slices (4 to 6 oz. each) fully cooked ham, halved
- ¼ cup thawed orange juice concentrate
- 2 Tbsp. brown sugar
- 1 tsp. prepared horseradish
- 1 tsp. grated orange zest
- Coarsely ground pepper

1. Grease two 15x10x1-in. baking pans with cooking spray. Add potatoes, carrots, turnip and onion; generously coat with cooking spray. Bake the vegetables, uncovered, at 425° until tender, 25-30 minutes.
2. Arrange ham slices over vegetables. In a bowl, combine concentrate, brown sugar, horseradish and orange zest. Spoon over ham and vegetables. Bake until the ham is heated through, about 10 minutes longer. Sprinkle with pepper.
1 serving: 375 cal., 5g fat (1g sat. fat), 71mg chol., 1179mg sod., 55g carb. (15g sugars, 7g fiber), 31g pro.

SLICED HAM WITH
ROASTED VEGETABLES

INDIVIDUAL
SHEPHERD'S PIES

SMOKY GRILLED PIZZA WITH GREENS & TOMATOES

This smoky grilled pizza scores big with me for two reasons: It encourages my husband and son to eat greens, and it showcases fresh produce.
—*Sarah Gray, Erie, CO*

PREP: 15 MIN. + RISING • **GRILL:** 10 MIN.
MAKES: 2 PIZZAS (4 PIECES EACH)

- 3 cups all-purpose flour
- 2 tsp. kosher salt
- 1 tsp. active dry yeast
- 3 Tbsp. olive oil, divided
- 1¼ to 1½ cups warm water (120° to 130°)

TOPPING

- 2 Tbsp. olive oil
- 10 cups beet greens, coarsely chopped
- 4 garlic cloves, minced
- 2 Tbsp. balsamic vinegar
- ¾ cup prepared pesto
- ¾ cup shredded Italian cheese blend
- ½ cup crumbled feta cheese
- 2 medium heirloom tomatoes, thinly sliced
- ¼ cup fresh basil leaves, chopped

1. Place flour, salt and yeast in a food processor; pulse until blended. While processing, add 2 Tbsp. oil and enough water in a steady stream for dough to form a ball. Turn dough onto a floured surface; knead until smooth and elastic, 6-8 minutes.

2. Place in a greased bowl, turning once to grease the top. Cover and let rise in a warm place until almost doubled, about 1½ hours.

3. Punch down dough. On a lightly floured surface, divide the dough into 2 portions. Press or roll each portion into a 10-in. circle; place each dough circle on a piece of greased foil (about 12 in. square). Brush tops with remaining oil; cover and let rest 10 minutes.

4. For topping, in a 6-qt. stockpot, heat oil over medium-high heat. Add beet greens; cook and stir until tender, 3-5 minutes. Add garlic; cook 30 seconds longer. Remove from heat; stir in vinegar.

5. Carefully invert pizza crusts onto oiled grill rack; remove foil. Grill, covered, over medium heat until bottoms are lightly browned, 3-5 minutes. Turn; grill until the second side begins to brown, 1-2 minutes.

6. Remove from grill. Spread with pesto; top with beet greens, cheeses and tomatoes. Return pizzas to the grill. Cook, covered, over medium heat until cheese is melted, 2-4 minutes. Sprinkle with basil.

1 piece: 407 cal., 20g fat (5g sat. fat), 11mg chol., 1007mg sod., 44g carb. (3g sugars, 4g fiber), 11g pro.

54

INDIVIDUAL SHEPHERD'S PIES

These savory muffin cup pies make a fun surprise for the family. Extras are easy to freeze and eat later on busy weeknights.
—*Ellen Osborne, Clarksville, TN*

PREP: 30 MIN. • **BAKE:** 20 MIN.
MAKES: 10 MINI PIES

- 1 lb. ground beef
- 3 Tbsp. chopped onion
- ½ tsp. minced garlic
- ⅓ cup chili sauce or ketchup
- 1 Tbsp. cider vinegar
- 2 cups hot mashed potatoes (with added milk and butter)
- 3 oz. cream cheese, softened
- 1 tube (12 oz.) refrigerated buttermilk biscuits
- ½ cup crushed potato chips
   Paprika, optional

1. Preheat oven to 375°. In a large skillet, cook beef and onion over medium heat until beef is no longer pink, 5-7 minutes, breaking up beef into crumbles. Add garlic; cook 1 minute or until tender. Drain. Stir in chili sauce and vinegar.
2. In a small bowl, mix mashed potatoes and cream cheese until blended. Press 1 biscuit onto the bottom and up sides of each of 10 greased muffin cups. Fill with beef mixture. Spread potato mixture over tops. Sprinkle with potato chips, pressing down lightly.
3. Bake until mini pies are golden brown, 20-25 minutes. If desired, sprinkle with paprika.
FREEZE OPTION: Freeze the cooled shepherd's pies in a single layer in freezer containers. To use, partially thaw in the refrigerator overnight. Bake on a baking sheet in a preheated 375° oven until heated through, 15-18 minutes.
2 mini pies: 567 cal., 30g fat (12g sat. fat), 84mg chol., 1378mg sod., 51g carb. (9g sugars, 2g fiber), 23g pro.

SERVE WITH:
Creamy Root
Veggie Soup,
Page 81

SHRIMP PUTTANESCA

I toss together these bold ingredients for a feisty seafood pasta.
—*Lynda Balslev, Sausalito, CA*

TAKES: 30 MIN. • **MAKES:** 4 SERVINGS

- 2 Tbsp. olive oil, divided
- 1 lb. uncooked shrimp (31-40 per lb.), peeled and deveined
- ¾ to 1 tsp. crushed red pepper flakes, divided
- ¼ tsp. salt
- 1 small onion, chopped
- 2 to 3 anchovy fillets, finely chopped
- 3 garlic cloves, minced
- 2 cups grape tomatoes or small cherry tomatoes
- ½ cup dry white wine or vegetable broth
- ⅓ cup pitted Greek olives, coarsely chopped
- 2 tsp. drained capers
  Sugar to taste
  Chopped fresh Italian parsley
  Hot cooked spaghetti, optional

1. In a large skillet, heat 1 Tbsp. oil; saute shrimp with ½ tsp. pepper flakes until shrimp turn pink, 2-3 minutes. Stir in salt; remove from pan.
2. In same pan, heat remaining oil over medium heat; saute onion until tender, about 2 minutes. Add anchovies, garlic and remaining pepper flakes; cook and stir until fragrant, about 1 minute. Stir in the tomatoes, wine, olives and capers; bring to a boil. Reduce the heat; simmer, uncovered, until tomatoes are softened and mixture is thickened, 8-10 minutes.
3. Stir in the shrimp. Add sugar to taste; sprinkle with parsley. If desired, serve with spaghetti.
1 cup shrimp mixture: 228 cal., 12g fat (2g sat. fat), 140mg chol., 579mg sod., 8g carb. (3g sugars, 1g fiber), 20g pro.

NEW ENGLAND BEAN
& BOG CASSOULET

NEW ENGLAND BEAN & BOG CASSOULET

When I moved to New England, I embraced the local cuisine. My cassoulet with baked beans pays tribute to both my new region and a French classic.
—*Devon Delaney, Westport, CT*

PREP: 15 MIN. • **COOK:** 35 MIN.
MAKES: 8 SERVINGS (3½ QT.)

- 5 Tbsp. olive oil, divided
- 8 boneless skinless chicken thighs (about 2 lbs.)
- 1 pkg. (12 oz.) fully cooked Italian chicken sausage links, cut into ½-in. slices
- 4 shallots, finely chopped
- 2 tsp. minced fresh rosemary or ½ tsp. dried rosemary, crushed
- 2 tsp. minced fresh thyme or ½ tsp. dried thyme
- 1 can (28 oz.) fire-roasted diced tomatoes, undrained
- 1 can (16 oz.) baked beans
- 1 cup chicken broth
- ½ cup fresh or frozen cranberries
- 3 day-old croissants, cubed (about 6 cups)
- ½ tsp. lemon-pepper seasoning
- 2 Tbsp. minced fresh parsley

1. Preheat oven to 400°. In a Dutch oven, heat 2 Tbsp. oil over medium heat. In batches, brown chicken thighs on both sides; remove from pan, reserving drippings. Add sausage; cook and stir until lightly browned. Remove from pan.
2. In same pan, heat 1 Tbsp. oil over medium heat. Add shallots, rosemary and thyme; cook and stir until shallots are tender, 1-2 minutes. Stir in tomatoes, beans, broth and cranberries. Return chicken and sausage to pan; bring to a boil. Bake, covered, until chicken is tender, 20-25 minutes.
3. Toss croissant pieces with remaining oil; sprinkle with lemon pepper. Arrange over chicken mixture. Bake, uncovered, until croissant pieces are golden brown, 12-15 minutes. Sprinkle with parsley.
1¾ cups: 500 cal., 26g fat (7g sat. fat), 127mg chol., 1050mg sod., 32g carb. (6g sugars, 5g fiber), 35g pro.

BALSAMIC BRAISED POT ROAST

SALMON WITH ROOT VEGETABLES

This cozy hash is loaded with protein and healthy fats that keep you going on busy days. We've been known to devour it at breakfast, lunch and dinner!
—*Courtney Stultz, Weir, KS*

TAKES: 25 MIN. • **MAKES:** 6 SERVINGS

- 2   Tbsp. olive oil
- 2   medium sweet potatoes, peeled and cut into ¼-in. cubes
- 2   medium red potatoes, cut into ¼-in. cubes
- 2   medium turnips, peeled and diced
- 2   medium carrots, peeled and diced
- 1   tsp. sea salt, divided
- 1   tsp. chili powder
- ¾   tsp. pepper, divided
- ½   tsp. ground cinnamon
- ½   tsp. ground cumin
- 6   salmon fillets (6 oz. each)

1. Preheat oven to 400°. In a large skillet, heat oil over medium heat. Add potatoes, turnips and carrots. Combine ½ tsp. salt, chili powder, ½ tsp. pepper, cinnamon and cumin; sprinkle over the vegetables. Cook, stirring frequently, until vegetables are tender, 15-20 minutes.
2. Meanwhile, place salmon, skin side down, in a foil-lined 15x10x1-in. baking pan. Sprinkle with the remaining ½ tsp. salt and ¼ tsp. pepper. Bake 10 minutes. Preheat broiler; broil just until the fish begins to flake easily, 2-5 minutes. Serve salmon with vegetables.
1 serving: 417 cal., 21g fat (4g sat. fat), 85mg chol., 464mg sod., 26g carb. (9g sugars, 4g fiber), 31g pro. **Diabetic exchanges:** 4 lean meat, 2 starch, 1 fat.

TEST KITCHEN TIP: A simple way to determine when salmon has finished cooking is to use the flake test: Press down on the top of the fillet with a fork. If the salmon flakes, or separates along the lines of its flesh, it's finished cooking. Its flesh should look opaque.

BALSAMIC BRAISED POT ROAST

Believe it or not, there is an art to the perfect pot roast. The classic dish is an easy, elegant way to serve a relatively inexpensive cut of meat. Every time I make it, my family gobbles it up.
—*Kelly Anderson, Glendale, CA*

PREP: 40 MIN. • **BAKE:** 2½ HOURS
MAKES: 8 SERVINGS

- 1   boneless beef chuck roast (3 to 4 lbs.)
- 1   tsp. salt
- ½   tsp. pepper
- 2   Tbsp. olive oil
- 3   celery ribs with leaves, cut into 2-in. pieces
- 2   medium carrots, cut into 1-in. pieces
- 1   medium onion, cut into wedges
- 3   medium turnips, peeled and quartered
- 1   large sweet potato, peeled and cubed
- 3   garlic cloves, minced
- 1   cup dry red wine or beef broth
- 1   can (14½ oz.) beef broth
- ½   cup balsamic vinegar
- 1   small bunch fresh thyme sprigs
- 4   fresh sage leaves
- 2   bay leaves
- ¼   cup cornstarch
- ¼   cup cold water

1. Preheat oven to 325°. Sprinkle roast with salt and pepper. In a Dutch oven, heat oil over medium heat. Brown roast on all sides. Remove from pot.
2. Add celery, carrots and onion to the pot; cook and stir 3-4 minutes or until fragrant. Add turnips, sweet potato and garlic; cook 1 minute longer.
3. Add wine, stirring to loosen browned bits from pot. Stir in broth, vinegar and herbs. Return roast to pot; bring to a boil. Bake, covered, 2½ to 3 hours or until meat is tender.
4. Remove beef and vegetables; keep warm. Discard herbs from cooking juices; skim off fat. In a small bowl, mix cornstarch and water until smooth; stir into cooking juices. Bring to a boil; cook and stir until thickened, about 2 minutes. Serve with pot roast and vegetables.
4 oz. cooked beef with 1 cup vegetables and ½ cup gravy: 405 cal., 20g fat (7g sat. fat), 111mg chol., 657mg sod., 19g carb. (9g sugars, 3g fiber), 35g pro.

CHAPTER 3

FAVORITE FARMHOUSE ENTREES

Few things celebrate the comfort of togetherness like a Sunday dinner with those you love. From golden roast chicken and succulent beef tenderloin to hearty meat pies and finger-licking ribs slathered in sauce, the down-home specialties found here promise to make memories around your table.

CHIPOTLE CITRUS-GLAZED
TURKEY TENDERLOINS

AUTUMN APPLE CHICKEN

I'd just been apple picking and wanted to bake something new with the bounty. Slow-cooking chicken with apples and barbecue sauce filled my whole house with the most delicious smell. We couldn't wait to eat.

—*Caitlyn Hauser, Brookline, NH*

PREP: 20 MIN. • **COOK:** 3½ HOURS
MAKES: 4 SERVINGS

- 1 **Tbsp. canola oil**
- 4 **bone-in chicken thighs (about 1½ lbs.), skin removed**
- ¼ **tsp. salt**
- ¼ **tsp. pepper**
- 2 **medium Fuji or Gala apples, coarsely chopped**
- 1 **medium onion, chopped**
- 1 **garlic clove, minced**
- ⅓ **cup barbecue sauce**
- ¼ **cup apple cider or juice**
- 1 **Tbsp. honey**

1. In a large skillet, heat oil over medium heat. Brown chicken thighs on both sides; sprinkle with salt and pepper. Transfer to a 3-qt. slow cooker; top with apples.
2. Add onion to same skillet; cook and stir over medium heat 2-3 minutes or until tender. Add garlic; cook 1 minute longer. Stir in barbecue sauce, apple cider and honey; increase the heat to medium-high. Cook 1 minute, stirring to loosen browned bits from pan. Pour over the chicken and apples. Cook, covered, on low 3½-4½ hours or until chicken is tender.
FREEZE OPTION: Freeze cooled chicken mixture in freezer containers. To use, partially thaw in refrigerator overnight. Heat through in a covered saucepan, stirring occasionally.
1 chicken thigh with ½ cup apple mixture: 333 cal., 13g fat (3g sat. fat), 87mg chol., 456mg sod., 29g carb. (22g sugars, 3g fiber), 25g pro. **Diabetic exchanges:** 4 lean meat, 1½ starch, ½ fruit.

CHIPOTLE CITRUS-GLAZED TURKEY TENDERLOINS

This simple skillet recipe makes it so easy to cook turkey on a weeknight. The combination of sweet, spicy and smoky flavors from orange, peppers and molasses is amazing.

—*Darlene Morris, Franklinton, LA*

TAKES: 30 MIN.
MAKES: 4 SERVINGS (½ CUP SAUCE)

- 4 **turkey breast tenderloins (5 oz. each)**
- ¼ **tsp. salt**
- ¼ **tsp. pepper**
- 1 **Tbsp. canola oil**
- ¾ **cup orange juice**
- ¼ **cup lime juice**
- ¼ **cup packed brown sugar**
- 1 **Tbsp. molasses**
- 2 **tsp. minced chipotle peppers in adobo sauce**
- 2 **Tbsp. minced fresh cilantro**

1. Sprinkle turkey with salt and pepper. In a large skillet, brown turkey in oil on all sides.
2. Meanwhile, in a small bowl whisk the juices, brown sugar, molasses and chipotle peppers; add to skillet. Reduce heat and simmer for 12-16 minutes or until turkey reaches 165°. Transfer turkey to a cutting board; let rest for 5 minutes.
3. Simmer glaze until thickened, about 4 minutes. Slice turkey and serve with glaze. Top with cilantro.
4 oz. cooked turkey with 2 Tbsp. glaze: 274 cal., 5g fat (0 sat. fat), 56mg chol., 252mg sod., 24g carb. (22g sugars, 0 fiber), 35g pro.

SERVE WITH:
Pumpkin &
Cauliflower Garlic
Mash, Page 82

CRUNCHY COATED WALLEYE

Potato flakes make a golden coating for these fish fillets, which are a breeze to fry on the stovetop.
—*Sondra Ostheimer, Boscobel, WI*

TAKES: 20 MIN. • **MAKES:** 4 SERVINGS

- ⅓ cup all-purpose flour
- 1 tsp. paprika
- ½ tsp. salt
- ¼ tsp. pepper
- ¼ tsp. onion powder
- ¼ tsp. garlic powder
- 2 large eggs
- 2¼ lbs. walleye, perch or pike fillets
- 1½ cups mashed potato flakes
- ⅓ cup vegetable oil
  Optional: Tartar sauce and lemon wedges

1. In a shallow bowl, combine flour, paprika, salt, pepper, onion powder and garlic powder. In another bowl, beat the eggs. Dip both sides of fillets in flour mixture and eggs, then coat with the potato flakes.
2. In a large skillet, fry fillets in oil for 5 minutes on each side or until fish flakes easily with a fork. Serve with tartar sauce and lemon if desired.
5 oz.-weight: 566 cal., 24g fat (4g sat. fat), 326mg chol., 508mg sod., 29g carb. (0 sugars, 2g fiber), 55g pro.

CHICKEN-STUFFED CUBANELLE PEPPERS

Here's a new take on traditional stuffed peppers. I substituted chicken for the beef and used Cubanelle peppers in place of the usual green peppers.
—*Bev Burlingame, Canton, OH*

PREP: 20 MIN. • **BAKE:** 1 HOUR
MAKES: 6 SERVINGS

- 6 Cubanelle peppers or mild banana peppers
- 2 large eggs, lightly beaten
- 3 cups shredded cooked chicken breast
- 1 cup salsa
- ¾ cup soft bread crumbs
- ½ cup cooked long grain rice
- 2 cups meatless pasta sauce

1. Preheat oven to 350°. Cut and discard tops from the peppers; remove seeds. In a large bowl, mix the eggs, chicken, salsa, bread crumbs and rice. Spoon into peppers.
2. Spread pasta sauce onto bottom of a 13x9-in. baking dish coated with cooking spray. Top with peppers. Bake, covered, 60-65 minutes or until peppers are tender and a thermometer inserted in stuffing reads at least 165°.
1 stuffed pepper: 230 cal., 4g fat (1g sat. fat), 125mg chol., 661mg sod., 20g carb. (7g sugars, 5g fiber), 26g pro. **Diabetic exchanges:** 3 lean meat, 2 vegetable, 1 starch.

CIDER-GLAZED HAM

Here is a heartwarming and classic way to serve ham. Apple cider and mustard accent the ham's rich, smoky flavor.
—*Jennifer Foos-Furer, Marysville, OH*

PREP: 15 MIN. • **COOK:** 4 HOURS
MAKES: 8 SERVINGS

- 1 boneless fully cooked ham (3 lbs.)
- 1¾ cups apple cider or juice
- ¼ cup packed brown sugar
- ¼ cup Dijon mustard
- ¼ cup honey
- 2 Tbsp. cornstarch
- 2 Tbsp. cold water

1. Place ham in a 5-qt. slow cooker. In a small bowl, combine the cider, brown sugar, mustard and honey; pour over the ham. Cover and cook on low for 4-5 hours or until heated through. Remove ham and keep warm.
2. Pour cooking juices into a small saucepan. Combine cornstarch and water until smooth; stir into cooking juices. Bring to a boil; cook and stir for 2 minutes or until thickened. Serve with the ham.
4 oz. cooked ham: 280 cal., 6g fat (2g sat. fat), 86mg chol., 1954mg sod., 26g carb. (21g sugars, 0 fiber), 31g pro.

GRILLED RIBEYES WITH BROWNED GARLIC BUTTER

Use the grill's smoke to flavor the ribeyes, then slather them with garlicky butter for a standout entree your friends and family will always remember.
—*Arge Salvatori, Waldwick, NJ*

TAKES: 25 MIN. • **MAKES:** 8 SERVINGS

- 6 Tbsp. unsalted butter, cubed
- 2 garlic cloves, minced
- 4 beef ribeye steaks (about 1 in. thick and 12 oz. each)
- 1½ tsp. salt
- 1½ tsp. pepper

1. In a small heavy saucepan, melt the butter with garlic over medium heat. Heat 4-6 minutes or until the butter is golden brown, stirring constantly. Remove from heat.
2. Season steaks with salt and pepper. Grill, covered, over medium heat or broil 4 in. from heat 5-7 minutes on each side or until the meat reaches desired doneness (for medium-rare, a thermometer should read 135°; medium, 140°; medium-well, 145°).
3. Gently warm the garlic butter over low heat. Serve with steaks.
4 oz. cooked beef with 2 tsp. garlic butter: 449 cal., 36g fat (16g sat. fat), 123mg chol., 521mg sod., 1g carb. (0 sugars, 0 fiber), 30g pro.

COUNTRY-FRIED STEAK

A healthier country-fried steak? Sounds like an oxymoron, but it's not. This dish keeps its classic comfort-food flavor while dropping over half the fat.
—Taste of Home *Test Kitchen*

PREP: 20 MIN. • **COOK:** 15 MIN.
MAKES: 4 SERVINGS

- 1 beef top round steak (1 lb.)
- ½ tsp. salt
- ½ tsp. garlic powder, divided
- ½ tsp. pepper, divided
- ¼ tsp. onion powder
- ½ cup buttermilk
- ¾ cup plus 4½ tsp. all-purpose flour, divided
- 1 Tbsp. canola oil
- 4½ tsp. butter
- 1 cup 2% milk

1. Cut steak into 4 serving-size pieces; pound to ¼-in. thickness. Combine the salt, ¼ tsp. garlic powder, ¼ tsp. pepper and onion powder; sprinkle over steaks.
2. Place buttermilk and ¾ cup flour in separate shallow bowls. Dip steaks in buttermilk, then flour.
3. In a large skillet, cook steaks in oil over medium heat for 3-4 minutes on each side or until meat is no longer pink. Remove and keep warm.
4. In a small saucepan, melt butter. Stir in the remaining flour until smooth; gradually add milk. Bring to a boil; cook and stir for 1 minute or until thickened. Stir in remaining garlic powder and pepper. Serve with steak.
1 serving: 318 cal., 13g fat (5g sat. fat), 80mg chol., 410mg sod., 19g carb. (4g sugars, 1g fiber), 30g pro.

CHICKEN & GOAT CHEESE SKILLET

My husband was completely bowled over by this on-a-whim skillet meal.
—*Ericka Barber, Eureka, CA*

TAKES: 20 MIN. • **MAKES:** 2 SERVINGS

- ½ lb. boneless skinless chicken breasts, cut into 1-in. pieces
- ¼ tsp. salt
- ⅛ tsp. pepper
- 2 tsp. olive oil
- 1 cup cut fresh asparagus (1-in. pieces)
- 1 garlic clove, minced
- 3 plum tomatoes, chopped
- 3 Tbsp. 2% milk
- 2 Tbsp. herbed fresh goat cheese, crumbled
  Hot cooked rice or pasta
  Additional goat cheese, optional

1. Toss the chicken with salt and pepper. In a large skillet, heat oil over medium-high heat; saute chicken until no longer pink, 4-6 minutes. Remove from pan; keep warm.
2. Add asparagus to skillet; cook and stir over medium-high heat 1 minute. Add garlic; cook and stir 30 seconds. Stir in tomatoes, milk and 2 Tbsp. cheese; cook, covered, over medium heat until cheese begins to melt, 2-3 minutes. Stir in chicken. Serve with rice. If desired, top with additional cheese.
1½ cups chicken mixture: 251 cal., 11g fat (3g sat. fat), 74mg chol., 447mg sod., 8g carb. (5g sugars, 3g fiber), 29g pro.
Diabetic exchanges: 4 lean meat, 2 fat, 1 vegetable.

APPLE BARBECUE CHICKEN

My husband and I had just moved to Dallas when I first made this recipe. Everything was new—new city, new home—but this dish felt familiar and comforting.
—Darla Andrews, Boerne, TX

TAKES: 30 MIN. • **MAKES:** 6 SERVINGS

- 12 chicken drumsticks
- ¼ tsp. pepper
- 1 Tbsp. olive oil
- 1 bottle (18 oz.) sweet and spicy barbecue sauce
- 2 cups applesauce
- ⅓ cup packed brown sugar
- 1 Tbsp. chili powder

1. Sprinkle drumsticks with pepper. In a Dutch oven, heat oil over medium heat. Brown drumsticks in batches; drain. Remove from pan.
2. Add remaining ingredients to pan, stirring to combine. Return chicken to pan; bring to a boil. Reduce heat; simmer, covered, 20-25 minutes or until chicken is tender.
2 chicken drumsticks with ½ cup sauce: 501 cal., 15g fat (4g sat. fat), 95mg chol., 949mg sod., 58g carb. (50g sugars, 1g fiber), 29g pro.

SERVE WITH:
Red, White & Blue
Summer Salad,
Page 75

APPLE ROASTED PORK WITH
CHERRY BALSAMIC GLAZE

APPLE ROASTED PORK WITH CHERRY BALSAMIC GLAZE

I added roasted apples, cherries and onions to turn ordinary pork for a meal-in-one dish, and I haven't turned back since. There is a short time frame between caramelized onions and burned ones, so pay close attention once they start cooking.
—Josh Downey, McHenry, IL

PREP: 30 MIN. • **BAKE:** 50 MIN+ STANDING
MAKES: 8 SERVINGS

- 1 boneless pork loin roast (3 lbs.)
- 1½ tsp. salt, divided
- ¾ tsp. pepper, divided
- ¼ cup olive oil, divided
- 3 medium apples, sliced
- 1½ cups unsweetened apple juice
- 6 medium onions, sliced (about 5 cups)
- 3 Tbsp. balsamic vinegar
- 1½ cups frozen pitted dark sweet cherries
- ½ cup cherry juice

1. Preheat oven to 350°. Sprinkle roast with 1 tsp. salt and ½ tsp. pepper. In an ovenproof Dutch oven, heat 2 Tbsp. oil over medium-high heat; brown roast on all sides. Add apples and apple juice to pan. Bake, uncovered, 50-60 minutes or until a thermometer inserted in pork reads 145°, basting occasionally with pan juices.
2. Meanwhile, in a large skillet, heat remaining oil over medium heat. Add onions and the remaining salt and pepper; cook and stir 8-10 minutes or until softened. Reduce heat to medium-low. Cook 35-40 minutes or until deep golden brown, stirring occasionally. Keep warm.
3. Remove the roast and apples to a serving plate; tent with foil. Let roast stand 10 minutes before slicing.
4. Skim fat from pork pan juices. Place over medium-high heat; add the vinegar and cook 1 minute, stirring to loosen browned bits from pan. Stir in cherries and cherry juice. Bring to a boil; cook 10-15 minutes or until the mixture is reduced to about 1 cup. Serve pork, apples and onions with cherry glaze.
1 serving: 387 cal., 15g fat (4g sat. fat), 85mg chol., 498mg sod., 29g carb. (20g sugars, 3g fiber), 34g pro.

SLOW-COOKED
BEEF BRISKET

TURKEY CURRY WITH RICE

When I have leftover turkey and a hankering for non-holiday food, I make turkey curry with carrots, cauliflower and mango chutney to spoon over rice.
—*Nancy Heishman, Las Vegas, NV*

TAKES: 30 MIN. • **MAKES:** 6 SERVINGS

- 1⅓ **cups chicken broth**
- 2 **Tbsp. curry powder**
- 2 **Tbsp. minced fresh cilantro**
- 3 **garlic cloves, minced**
- ¾ **tsp. salt**
- ½ **tsp. ground cardamom**
- ½ **tsp. pepper**
- 3 **medium carrots, thinly sliced**
- 1 **medium onion, finely chopped**
- 1 **pkg. (16 oz.) frozen cauliflower, thawed**
- 3 **cups chopped cooked turkey**
- ½ **cup mango chutney**
- 2 **tsp. all-purpose flour**
- 1 **cup coconut milk**
- 4½ **cups hot cooked rice**
  Additional mango chutney, optional

1. In a large saucepan, mix the first 7 ingredients. Add carrots and onion; bring to a boil. Reduce heat; simmer, covered, 3-5 minutes or until carrots are crisp-tender. Add cauliflower; cook, covered, 4-6 minutes longer or until vegetables are tender.
2. Stir in turkey and chutney; heat through. In a small bowl, mix flour and coconut milk until smooth; stir into turkey mixture. Bring to a boil, stirring constantly; cook and stir 1-2 minutes or until slightly thickened. Serve with rice and, if desired, additional chutney.
1 cup turkey mixture with ¾ cup rice: 363 cal., 9g fat (7g sat. fat), 1mg chol., 787mg sod., 64g carb. (16g sugars, 5g fiber), 7g pro.

SLOW-COOKED BEEF BRISKET

One bite of this super tender brisket, and your family will be hooked! The rich gravy is perfect for spooning over a side of creamy mashed potatoes.
—*Eunice Stoen, Decorah, IA*

PREP: 15 MIN. • **COOK:** 8 HOURS
MAKES: 6 SERVINGS

- 1 **fresh beef brisket (2½ to 3 lbs.)**
- 2 **tsp. liquid smoke, optional**
- 1 **tsp. celery salt**
- ½ **tsp. pepper**
- ¼ **tsp. salt**
- 1 **large onion, sliced**
- 1 **can (12 oz.) beer or nonalcoholic beer**
- 2 **tsp. Worcestershire sauce**
- 2 **Tbsp. cornstarch**
- ¼ **cup cold water**

1. Cut brisket in half; rub with liquid smoke, if desired, and celery salt, pepper and salt. Place in a 3-qt. slow cooker. Top with onion. Combine the beer and Worcestershire sauce; pour over meat. Cover and cook on low for 8-9 hours or until tender.
2. Remove brisket and keep warm. Strain the cooking juices; transfer to a small saucepan. In a small bowl, combine cornstarch and water until smooth; stir into juices. Bring to a boil; cook and stir until thickened, about 2 minutes. Serve beef with gravy.
5 oz. cooked brisket with about ⅓ cup sauce: 285 cal., 8g fat (3g sat. fat), 80mg chol., 430mg sod., 7g carb. (3g sugars, 0 fiber), 39g pro. **Diabetic exchanges:** 5 lean meat, ½ starch.

SERVE WITH:
Chive Smashed
Potatoes,
Page 78

APPLE & WALNUT
STUFFED PORK
TENDERLOIN
WITH RED
CURRANT SAUCE

APPLE & WALNUT STUFFED PORK TENDERLOIN WITH RED CURRANT SAUCE

My roasted pork tenderloin is stuffed with two of our favorite ingredients: walnuts and apples. This comforting entree is my family's most-requested pork dish.
—*Gloria Bradley, Naperville, IL*

PREP: 35 MIN. • **BAKE:** 55 MIN.
MAKES: 6 SERVINGS

- 1 Tbsp. butter
- 1 cup chopped walnuts
- 1 medium apple, peeled and finely chopped
- 3 Tbsp. dried cranberries
- 1 Tbsp. minced fresh parsley
- 1 Tbsp. olive oil
- 1 garlic clove, minced
- 1 pork tenderloin (1½ lbs.)
- ⅓ cup apple butter
- ½ tsp. salt
- ½ tsp. ground coriander

SAUCE
- 1 cup red currant jelly
- 1 shallot, finely chopped
- 2 Tbsp. cranberry juice
- 2 Tbsp. honey
- 1 Tbsp. dried currants
- 1 Tbsp. cider vinegar

1. In a large heavy skillet, melt butter. Add walnuts; cook and stir over medium heat until toasted, about 2 minutes. Remove ½ cup for serving. Add apple to the remaining walnuts; cook and stir 1 minute longer. Cool slightly.
2. Place cranberries, parsley, oil, garlic and apple mixture in a food processor; cover and process until finely chopped.
3. Cut a lengthwise slit down the center of the roast to within ½ in. of bottom. Open roast so it lies flat; cover with plastic wrap. Flatten to ½-in. thickness. Remove wrap; spread apple butter on 1 long side of tenderloin to within ¼ in. of edges. Top with apple mixture. Close meat; tie with kitchen string. Place on a rack in a shallow roasting pan; rub with salt and coriander.
4. Bake at 350° until a thermometer inserted into center of stuffing reads 165° and thermometer inserted in pork reads at least 145°, 55-65 minutes. Let stand for 10 minutes before slicing.
5. In a small saucepan, combine the sauce ingredients; bring to a boil. Reduce heat; simmer, uncovered, until slightly thickened, 12-14 minutes. Serve with the pork; top with reserved walnuts.
3 oz. cooked pork with 3 Tbsp. sauce: 513 cal., 21g fat (4g sat. fat), 68mg chol., 260mg sod., 59g carb. (51g sugars, 2g fiber), 26g pro.

BEEF TENDERLOIN WITH ROASTED VEGETABLES

I appreciate this recipe because it includes a side dish of roasted potatoes, Brussels sprouts and carrots. I prepare this entree for celebrations throughout the year.
—*Janet Singleton, Bellevue, OH*

PREP: 20 MIN. + MARINATING
BAKE: 1 HOUR + STANDING
MAKES: 10 SERVINGS

- 1 beef tenderloin roast (3 lbs.)
- ¾ cup dry white wine or beef broth
- ¾ cup reduced-sodium soy sauce
- 4 tsp. minced fresh rosemary
- 4 tsp. Dijon mustard
- 1½ tsp. ground mustard
- 3 garlic cloves, peeled and sliced
- 1 lb. Yukon Gold potatoes, cut into 1-in. wedges
- 1 lb. Brussels sprouts, halved
- 1 lb. fresh baby carrots

1. Place tenderloin in a large shallow dish. Combine the wine, soy sauce, rosemary, Dijon mustard, ground mustard and garlic. Pour half of the marinade over the tenderloin and turn to coat. Cover and refrigerate for 4-12 hours, turning several times. Cover and refrigerate remaining marinade.
2. Place the potatoes, Brussels sprouts and carrots in a greased 13x9-in. baking dish; add the reserved marinade and toss to coat. Cover and bake at 425° for 20 minutes; stir.
3. Drain tenderloin, discarding marinade; if desired, tie tenderloin with baker's twine. Place tenderloin over vegetables. Bake, uncovered, for 40-50 minutes or until meat reaches desired doneness (for medium-rare, a thermometer should read 135°; medium, 140°; medium-well, 145°).
4. Remove the beef and let stand for 15 minutes. Check vegetables for doneness. If additional roasting is needed, cover with foil and bake for 10-15 minutes or until tender. Slice beef and serve with vegetables.
1 serving: 283 cal., 8g fat (3g sat. fat), 60mg chol., 627mg sod., 16g carb. (4g sugars, 3g fiber), 33g pro. **Diabetic exchanges:** 4 lean meat, 1 vegetable, ½ starch.

BEEF TENDERLOIN WITH ROASTED VEGETABLES

PRETZEL-CRUSTED CATFISH

I'm not a big fish lover, so any concoction that has me enjoying fish is a keeper in my book. This combination of flavors works for me. It's awesome served with corn muffins, butter and honey!
—*Kelly Williams, Forked River, NJ*

TAKES: 30 MIN. • **MAKES:** 4 SERVINGS

- 4   catfish fillets (6 oz. each)
- ½   tsp. salt
- ½   tsp. pepper
- 2   large eggs
- ⅓   cup Dijon mustard
- 2   Tbsp. 2% milk
- ½   cup all-purpose flour
- 4   cups honey mustard miniature pretzels, coarsely crushed
     Oil for frying
     Lemon slices, optional

1. Sprinkle catfish with salt and pepper. Whisk the eggs, mustard and milk in a shallow bowl. Place flour and pretzels in separate shallow bowls. Coat fillets with flour, then dip in egg mixture and coat with pretzels.

2. Heat ¼ in. oil to 375° in an electric skillet. Fry fillets, a few at a time, until fish flakes easily with a fork, 3-4 minutes on each side. Drain on paper towels. Serve with lemon slices if desired.

1 fillet: 610 cal., 31g fat (4g sat. fat),164mg chol.,1579mg sod., 44g carb. (2g sugars, 2g fiber), 33g pro.

SERVE WITH:
Smoky Macaroni
& Cheese,
Page 89

PRETZEL-CRUSTED CATFISH

PEACH-GLAZED RIBS

For a mouthwatering alternative to the usual barbecue sauce for ribs, try this slightly spicy recipe at your next picnic. The peaches add just the right touch of sweetness and a lovely color to this special sauce.
—*Sharon Taylor, Columbia, SC*

PREP: 15 MIN. • **GRILL:** 1¼ HOURS
MAKES: 6 SERVINGS

3 to 4 lbs. pork baby back ribs, cut into serving-size pieces
1 can (15¼ oz.) peach halves, drained
⅓ cup soy sauce
¼ cup canola oil
¼ cup honey
2 Tbsp. brown sugar
1 tsp. sesame seeds, toasted
1 garlic clove, peeled
¼ tsp. ground ginger

1. Prepare grill for indirect heat, using a drip pan. Place ribs over drip pan. Grill, covered, over indirect medium heat for 60 minutes, turning occasionally.
2. Meanwhile, in a blender, combine remaining ingredients; cover and process until smooth. Baste ribs.
3. Grill until meat is tender and juices run clear, 15-20 minutes longer, basting occasionally with remaining sauce.
1 serving: 568 cal., 40g fat (13g sat. fat), 122mg chol., 930mg sod., 25g carb. (23g sugars, 1g fiber), 28g pro.

GRANDMA'S SWEDISH MEATBALLS

My mother made these hearty meatballs when we were growing up, and now my kids love them, too.
—*Karin Ness, Big Lake, MN*

TAKES: 30 MIN. • **MAKES:** 4 SERVINGS

1 large egg, lightly beaten
½ cup crushed saltines (about 10 crackers)
¼ tsp. seasoned salt
¼ tsp. pepper
½ lb. ground beef
½ lb. bulk pork sausage
¼ cup plus 2 Tbsp. all-purpose flour, divided
2½ cups reduced-sodium beef broth, divided
Hot mashed potatoes
Minced fresh parsley, optional

1. Mix first 4 ingredients. Add beef and sausage; mix lightly but thoroughly. Shape into 1-in. balls; toss with ¼ cup flour, coating lightly.
2. In a large skillet, brown meatballs over medium-high heat. Add 2 cups broth; bring to a boil. Reduce heat; simmer, covered, until meatballs are cooked through, 5-6 minutes.
3. Remove meatballs with a slotted spoon. Mix the remaining flour and broth until smooth; add to pan. Bring to a boil; cook and stir until thickened, 1-2 minutes. Return meatballs to pan; heat through. Serve meatballs with mashed potatoes. If desired, sprinkle with parsley.
1 serving: 348 cal., 21g fat (7g sat. fat), 115mg chol., 846mg sod., 17g carb. (1g sugars, 1g fiber), 21g pro.

MEATBALL CHILI
WITH DUMPLINGS

MEATBALL CHILI WITH DUMPLINGS

My family enjoys this delicious recipe—it's like a spicy meatball stew with dumplings!
—*Sarah Yoder, Middlebury, IN*

PREP: 20 MIN. • **COOK:** 50 MIN.
MAKES: 6 SERVINGS

- 1 large egg, beaten
- ¾ cup finely chopped onion, divided
- ¼ cup dry bread crumbs or rolled oats
- 5 tsp. beef bouillon granules, divided
- 3 tsp. chili powder, divided
- 1 lb. ground beef
- 3 Tbsp. all-purpose flour
- 1 Tbsp. canola oil
- 1 can (28 oz.) diced tomatoes, undrained
- 1 garlic clove, minced
- ½ tsp. ground cumin
- 1 can (16 oz.) kidney beans, rinsed and drained

CORNMEAL DUMPLINGS
- 1½ cups biscuit/baking mix
- ½ cup yellow cornmeal
- ⅔ cup 2% milk
- Minced chives, optional

1. In a large bowl, combine egg, ¼ cup onion, bread crumbs, 3 tsp. bouillon and 1 tsp. chili powder; crumble beef over mixture and mix lightly but thoroughly. Shape into twelve 1½-in. meatballs. Roll in flour.
2. Heat oil in a 12-in. cast-iron or other ovenproof skillet; brown meatballs. Drain on paper towels. Carefully wipe the skillet clean with paper towels. Add tomatoes, garlic, cumin and the remaining onion, bouillon and chili powder to skillet; stir to combine. Add meatballs. Cover and cook over low heat about 20 minutes. Stir in beans.
3. Combine dumpling ingredients. Drop by spoonfuls onto chili; cook on low, uncovered, for 10 minutes. Cover and cook until a toothpick inserted in a dumpling comes out clean, 10-12 minutes longer. If desired, sprinkle with minced chives.
1 serving: 475 cal., 16g fat (6g sat. fat), 76mg chol., 1523mg sod., 56g carb. (8g sugars, 7g fiber), 26g pro.

CITRUS-HERB ROAST CHICKEN

CITRUS-HERB ROAST CHICKEN

This dish is one of my all-time favorites. The flavorful, juicy chicken combines with the aromas of spring in fresh herbs, lemon and onions to form the perfect one-pot meal. I make the gravy right in the pan.
—*Megan Fordyce, Fairchance, PA*

PREP: 25 MIN. • **BAKE:** 2 HOURS + STANDING
MAKES: 8 SERVINGS

- 6 garlic cloves
- 1 roasting chicken (6 to 7 lbs.)
- 3 lbs. baby red potatoes, halved
- 6 medium carrots, halved lengthwise and cut into 1-in. pieces
- 4 fresh thyme sprigs
- 4 fresh dill sprigs
- 2 fresh rosemary sprigs
- 1 medium lemon
- 1 small navel orange
- 1 tsp. salt
- ½ tsp. pepper
- 3 cups chicken broth, warmed
- 6 green onions, cut into 2-in. pieces

1. Preheat oven to 350°. Peel and cut garlic into quarters. Place the chicken on a cutting board. Tuck wings under chicken. With a sharp paring knife, cut 24 small slits in breasts, drumsticks and thighs. Insert garlic in slits. Tie drumsticks together.
2. Place potatoes and carrots in a shallow roasting pan; top with herbs. Place chicken, breast side up, over vegetables and herbs. Cut lemon and orange in half; gently squeeze juices over chicken and vegetables. Place squeezed fruits inside chicken cavity. Sprinkle chicken with salt and pepper. Pour broth around chicken.
3. Roast until a thermometer inserted in thickest part of thigh reads 170°-175°, 2-2½ hours, sprinkling green onions over vegetables during last 20 minutes. (Cover loosely with foil if chicken browns too quickly.)
4. Remove chicken from oven; tent with foil. Let stand 15 minutes before carving. Discard herbs. If desired, skim fat and thicken pan drippings for gravy. Serve gravy with chicken and vegetables.
7 oz. cooked chicken with 1¼ cups vegetables: 561 cal., 24g fat (7g sat. fat) 136mg chol., 826mg sod., 39g carb. (5g sugars, 5g fiber), 47g pro.

CHAPTER 4
COUNTRY SIDES, SALADS & MORE

From garden-fresh salads and harvesttime sides to buttery breads
and heartwarming soups, the farmhouse recipes found here
make for a chapter you'll turn to time and again.

RED, WHITE &
BLUE SUMMER
SALAD

RED, WHITE & BLUE SUMMER SALAD

Caprese and fresh fruit always remind me of summer. In this salad, I combine traditional Caprese flavors with summer blueberries and peaches. I also add prosciutto for saltiness, creating a balanced, flavor-packed side dish.
—*Emily Falke, Santa Barbara, CA*

TAKES: 25 MIN. • **MAKES:** 12 SERVINGS

- ⅔ cup extra virgin olive oil
- ½ cup julienned fresh basil
- ⅓ cup white balsamic vinegar
- ¼ cup julienned fresh mint leaves
- 2 garlic cloves, minced
- 2 tsp. Dijon mustard
- 1 tsp. sea salt
- 1 tsp. sugar
- 1 tsp. pepper
- 2 cups cherry tomatoes
- 8 cups fresh arugula
- 1 carton (8 oz.) fresh mozzarella cheese pearls, drained
- 2 medium peaches, sliced
- 2 cups fresh blueberries
- 6 oz. thinly sliced prosciutto, julienned
  Additional mint leaves

1. In a small bowl, whisk the first 9 ingredients. Add tomatoes; let stand while preparing salad.
2. In a large bowl, combine arugula, mozzarella, peach slices, blueberries and prosciutto. Pour tomato mixture over top; toss to coat. Garnish with additional mint leaves. Serve salad immediately.
1 cup: 233 cal., 18g fat (5g sat. fat), 27mg chol., 486mg sod., 10g carb. (8g sugars, 2g fiber), 8g pro.

KITCHEN TIP: Using white balsamic vinegar keeps the colors bright in this sweet-salty salad.

SIMPLE AU GRATIN POTATOES

SIMPLE AU GRATIN POTATOES

These cheesy potatoes are always welcome at our dinner table, and they're so simple to make. A perfect complement to ham, the versatile, comforting side dish also goes well with pork, chicken and other entrees.
—*Cris O'Brien, Virginia Beach, VA*

PREP: 20 MIN. • **BAKE:** 1½ HOURS
MAKES: 8 SERVINGS

- 3 Tbsp. butter
- 3 Tbsp. all-purpose flour
- 1½ tsp. salt
- ⅛ tsp. pepper
- 2 cups 2% milk
- 1 cup shredded cheddar cheese
- 5 cups thinly sliced peeled potatoes (about 6 medium)
- ½ cup chopped onion
  Additional pepper, optional

1. Preheat oven to 350°. In a large saucepan, melt butter over low heat. Stir in flour, salt and pepper until smooth. Gradually add milk. Bring to a boil; cook and stir 2 minutes or until thickened. Remove from heat; stir in the cheese until melted. Add potatoes and onion.
2. Transfer mixture to a greased 2-qt baking dish. Cover and bake 1 hour. Uncover; bake 30-40 minutes or until the potatoes are tender. If desired, top with additional pepper.
¾ cup: 224 cal., 10g fat (7g sat. fat), 35mg chol., 605mg sod., 26g carb. (4g sugars, 2g fiber), 7g pro.

SERVE WITH:
Maple-Glazed Ham,
Page 7

MOM'S SWEET
POTATO BAKE

EASY BATTER ROLLS

The first thing my guests always ask when they come for dinner is whether or not I'm serving these dinner rolls. The buns are so light, airy and delicious that I'm constantly asked for the recipe.
—*Thomasina Brunner, Gloversville, NY*

PREP: 30 MIN. + RISING • **BAKE:** 15 MIN.
MAKES: 1 DOZEN

- 3 cups all-purpose flour
- 2 Tbsp. sugar
- 1 pkg. (¼ oz.) active dry yeast
- 1 tsp. salt
- 1 cup water
- 2 Tbsp. butter
- 1 large egg, room temperature
  Melted butter

1. In a large bowl, combine 2 cups flour, sugar, yeast and salt. In a saucepan, heat water and butter to 120°-130°. Add to dry ingredients; beat until blended. Add egg; beat on low speed for 30 seconds, then on high for 3 minutes. Stir in enough of the remaining flour to form a stiff dough. Do not knead. Cover and let rise in a warm place until doubled, about 30 minutes.
2. Stir dough down. Fill 12 greased muffin cups half full. Cover and let rise until doubled, about 15 minutes.
3. Bake at 350° until golden brown, 15-20 minutes. Cool for 1 minute before removing from pan to a wire rack. Brush tops with melted butter.
FREEZE OPTION: Freeze the cooled rolls in airtight containers. To use, microwave each roll on high until warmed through, 30-45 seconds.
1 roll: 147 cal., 3g fat (1g sat. fat), 21mg chol., 219mg sod., 26g carb. (2g sugars, 1g fiber), 4g pro.

SERVE WITH:
Spinach & Tortellini
Soup,
Page 83

MOM'S SWEET POTATO BAKE

Mom loves sweet potatoes and fixed them often in this creamy, comforting casserole. With its nutty topping, this side dish could almost serve as a dessert. It's a real treat!
—*Sandi Pichon, Memphis, TN*

PREP: 10 MIN. • **BAKE:** 45 MIN.
MAKES: 8 SERVINGS

- 3 cups cold mashed sweet potatoes (prepared without milk or butter)
- 1 cup sugar
- 3 large eggs
- ½ cup 2% milk
- ¼ cup butter, softened
- 1 tsp. salt
- 1 tsp. vanilla extract

TOPPING
- ½ cup packed brown sugar
- ½ cup chopped pecans
- ¼ cup all-purpose flour
- 2 Tbsp. cold butter

1. Preheat oven to 325°. In a large bowl, beat the sweet potatoes, sugar, eggs, milk, butter, salt and vanilla until smooth. Transfer to a greased 2-qt. baking dish.
2. In a small bowl, combine the brown sugar, pecans and flour; cut in butter until crumbly. Sprinkle over the sweet potato mixture. Bake, uncovered, until a thermometer reads 160°, 45-50 minutes.
½ cup: 417 cal., 16g fat (7g sat. fat), 94mg chol., 435mg sod., 65g carb. (47g sugars, 4g fiber), 6g pro.

CHIVE SMASHED POTATOES

No need to peel the potatoes—in fact, this is the only way we make mashed potatoes anymore. Mixing in the flavored cream cheese is a delightful twist.
—*Beverly A. Norris, Evanston, WY*

TAKES: 30 MIN. • **MAKES:** 12 SERVINGS

- 4 lbs. red potatoes, quartered
- 2 tsp. chicken bouillon granules
- 1 carton (8 oz.) spreadable chive and onion cream cheese
- ½ cup half-and-half cream
- ¼ cup butter, cubed
- 1 tsp. salt
- ¼ tsp. pepper
  Chopped chives, optional

1. Place potatoes and bouillon in a Dutch oven and cover with 8 cups water. Bring to a boil. Reduce heat; cover and cook until tender, 15-20 minutes.
2. Drain and return to pan. Mash the potatoes with cream cheese, cream, butter, salt and pepper. If desired, garnish with chives.
⅔ cup: 219 cal., 11g fat (7g sat. fat), 31mg chol., 428mg sod., 26g carb. (3g sugars, 3g fiber), 5g pro.

RED & GREEN SALAD WITH TOASTED ALMONDS

RED & GREEN SALAD WITH TOASTED ALMONDS

During a long Midwest winter, I crave greens and tomatoes from the garden. This salad has a fantastic out-of-the-garden taste. Thank goodness I can get the ingredients all year-round.
—*Jasmine Rose, Crystal Lake, IL*

TAKES: 25 MIN.
MAKES: 12 SERVINGS (1⅓ CUPS EACH)

- ¼ cup red wine vinegar
- 1 Tbsp. reduced-sodium soy sauce
- 2 garlic cloves, minced
- 2 tsp. sesame oil
- 2 tsp. honey
- 1 tsp. minced fresh gingerroot or ½ tsp. ground ginger
- ⅛ tsp. Louisiana-style hot sauce
- ½ cup grapeseed or canola oil

SALAD
- 2 heads Boston or Bibb lettuce, torn
- 1 head red leaf lettuce
- 1 medium sweet red pepper, julienned
- 2 celery ribs, sliced
- 1 cup sliced English cucumber
- 1 cup frozen peas, thawed
- 1 cup grape tomatoes, halved
- 1 cup sliced almonds, toasted

1. In a small bowl, whisk the first 7 ingredients. Gradually whisk in the grapeseed oil until blended.
2. In a large bowl, combine lettuces, red pepper, celery, cucumber, peas and tomatoes. Just before serving, pour dressing over salad and toss to coat. Sprinkle with almonds.
1⅓ cups: 168 cal., 14g fat (1g sat. fat), 0 chol., 90mg sod., 8g carb. (3g sugars, 3g fiber), 4g pro. **Diabetic exchanges:** 3 fat, 1 vegetable.

ZUCCHINI
IN DILL
CREAM SAUCE

HERBED HARVEST VEGETABLE CASSEROLE

I belong to a cooking club, so I try a lot of new recipes. This one has become one of my favorites. I hope your family enjoys it as much as mine does!
—*Netty Dyck, St. Catharines, ON*

PREP: 15 MIN.
BAKE: 1 HOUR 40 MIN. + STANDING
MAKES: 6-8 SERVINGS

- 4   new potatoes, cut in ¼-in. slices
- ¼   cup butter
- 1   Tbsp. finely chopped fresh sage or 1 tsp. dried sage
- 1   Tbsp. finely chopped fresh tarragon or 1 tsp. dried tarragon
- 3   sweet red bell peppers, seeded and diced
- 1   onion, thinly sliced
- ½   cup uncooked long-grain rice
- 3   medium zucchini, thinly sliced
- 4   medium tomatoes, sliced
- 1   cup shredded Swiss cheese

1. Grease a 2½-qt. baking dish and arrange half the potato slices in overlapping rows. Dot with half the butter. Sprinkle with half the sage, tarragon, peppers, onion, rice and zucchini. Dot with remaining butter and repeat layering.
2. Cover and bake at 350° for 1½ hours or until potatoes are tender. Uncover; top with tomato slices and cheese. Bake 10 minutes longer or until tomatoes are warm and cheese is melted. Remove from oven; cover and let stand for 10 minutes before serving.
1 serving: 206 cal., 10g fat (6g sat. fat), 28mg chol.,105mg sod., 24g carb. (6g sugars, 4g fiber), 7g pro.

ZUCCHINI IN DILL CREAM SAUCE

We were dairy farmers until we retired in 1967, so I always use fresh, real dairy products in my recipes. This creamy sauce combines all of our favorite foods!
—*Josephine Vanden Heuvel, Hart, MI*

TAKES: 30 MIN. • **MAKES:** 8 SERVINGS

- 7   cups sliced zucchini (¼-in. slices)
- ¼   cup finely chopped onion
- ½   cup water
- 1   tsp. salt
- 1   tsp. chicken bouillon granules or 1 chicken bouillon cube
- ½   tsp. dill weed
- 2   Tbsp. butter, melted
- 2   tsp. sugar
- 1   tsp. lemon juice
- 2   Tbsp. all-purpose flour
- ¼   cup sour cream

1. In Dutch oven, combine the zucchini, onion, water, salt, bouillon and dill; bring to a boil. Add the butter, sugar and lemon juice; mix. Remove from the heat; do not drain.
2. Combine flour and sour cream; stir half the mixture into hot zucchini. Return to heat; add remaining cream mixture and cook until thickened.
¾ cup: 73 cal., 4g fat,11mg chol., 419mg sod., 8g carb., 2g pro. **Diabetic exchanges:** 1 vegetable, 1 fat.

♥
SERVE WITH:
Tuscan
Fish Packets,
Page 43

BAKED BEANS MOLE

My son and husband love this hearty side dish that is quick and easy to prepare but yet so flavorful. Chocolate, chili and honey mingle to create a rich, savory flavor that's not too spicy and not too sweet.
—*Roxanne Chan, Albany, CA*

PREP: 25 MIN. • **BAKE:** 40 MINUTES
MAKES: 8 SERVINGS

¼ lb. fresh chorizo, crumbled
½ cup chopped onion
½ cup chopped sweet red pepper
1 large garlic clove, minced
1 can (15 oz.) black beans, rinsed and drained
1 can (15 oz.) pinto beans, rinsed and drained
1 can (15 oz.) black-eyed peas, rinsed and drained
1 cup salsa (medium or hot)
1 cup chili sauce
2 Tbsp. honey
1 Tbsp. instant coffee granules
½ tsp. ground cinnamon
2 oz. chopped bittersweet or semisweet chocolate
Minced fresh cilantro

Preheat oven to 375°. In a large, ovenproof skillet with a lid, cook chorizo, onion, red pepper and garlic over medium heat until sausage is browned, 4-6 minutes. Add next the 9 ingredients; mix well. Bake, covered, until thickened and flavors are blended, about 40 minutes. Sprinkle with cilantro.
⅔ cup: 284 cal., 7g fat (3g sat. fat), 13mg chol., 989mg sod., 40g carb. (14g sugars, 6g fiber), 11g pro.

KITCHEN TIPS: Although this dish is delicious with several different types of beans, it would be equally good with just one. You can also add 2-3 cups of broth to make a festive mole chili.

SERVE WITH:
Best-Ever
Fried Chicken,
Page 11

**CREAMY ROOT
VEGGIE SOUP**

CREAMY ROOT VEGGIE SOUP

On chilly nights, we fill the pot with parsnips and celery root for a smooth, creamy soup. Garlic, bacon and fresh thyme make it even better.
—*Sally Sibthorpe, Shelby Township, MI*

PREP: 15 MIN. • **COOK:** 1 HOUR
MAKES: 8 SERVINGS

- 4 bacon strips, chopped
- 1 large onion, chopped
- 3 garlic cloves, minced
- 1 large celery root, peeled and cubed (about 5 cups)
- 6 medium parsnips, peeled and cubed (about 4 cups)
- 6 cups chicken stock
- 1 bay leaf
- 1 cup heavy whipping cream
- 2 tsp. minced fresh thyme
- 1 tsp. salt
- ¼ tsp. white pepper
- ¼ tsp. ground nutmeg
  Additional minced fresh thyme

1. In a Dutch oven, cook the bacon over medium heat until crisp, stirring occasionally. Remove with a slotted spoon; drain on paper towels. Cook and stir onion in bacon drippings 6-8 minutes or until tender. Add the garlic; cook 1 minute longer.
2. Add celery root, parsnips, stock and bay leaf. Bring to a boil. Reduce heat; cook, uncovered, 30-40 minutes or until vegetables are tender. Remove bay leaf.
3. Puree soup using an immersion blender. Or, cool slightly and puree in batches in a blender; return to pan. Stir in cream, 2 tsp. thyme, salt, pepper and nutmeg; heat through. Top servings with bacon and additional thyme.
1 cup: 295 cal., 17g fat (9g sat. fat), 50mg chol., 851mg sod., 30g carb. (9g sugars, 6g fiber), 8g pro.

HERB QUICK BREAD

This simple bread is especially good with soups and stews, but slices are also tasty alongside fresh, green salads. Try it for sandwiches, too. The herbs make it a flavorful treat any time.
—*Donna Roberts, Manhattan, KS*

PREP: 15 MIN. • **BAKE:** 40 MIN. + COOLING
MAKES: 1 LOAF (16 PIECES)

- 3 cups all-purpose flour
- 3 Tbsp. sugar
- 1 Tbsp. baking powder
- 3 tsp. caraway seeds
- ½ tsp. salt
- ½ tsp. ground nutmeg
- ½ tsp. dried thyme
- 1 large egg, room temperature
- 1 cup fat-free milk
- ⅓ cup canola oil

1. Preheat oven to 350°. In a large bowl, whisk together first 7 ingredients. In another bowl, whisk together egg, milk and oil. Add to flour mixture; stir just until moistened.
2. Transfer to a 9x5-in. loaf pan coated with cooking spray. Bake until a toothpick inserted in center comes out clean, 40-50 minutes. Cool in pan 10 minutes before removing to a wire rack to cool.
1 piece: 147 cal., 5g fat (1g sat. fat), 12mg chol., 160mg sod., 21g carb. (3g sugars, 1g fiber), 3g pro. **Diabetic exchanges:** 1½ starch, 1 fat.

PUMPKIN & CAULIFLOWER GARLIC MASH

I wanted healthy alternatives to my family's favorite recipes. Pumpkin, cauliflower and thyme make an amazing dish. You'll never miss those plain old mashed potatoes.
—*Kari Wheaton, South Beloit, IL*

TAKES: 25 MIN. • **MAKES:** 6 SERVINGS

- 1 medium head cauliflower, broken into florets (about 6 cups)
- 3 garlic cloves
- ⅓ cup spreadable cream cheese
- 1 can (15 oz.) solid-pack pumpkin
- 1 Tbsp. minced fresh thyme
- 1 tsp. salt
- ¼ tsp. cayenne pepper
- ¼ tsp. pepper

1. Place 1 in. of water in a Dutch oven; bring to a boil. Add the cauliflower and garlic cloves; cook, covered, until tender, 8-10 minutes. Drain; carefully transfer to a food processor.
2. Add remaining ingredients; process until smooth. Return to pan; heat through, stirring occasionally.
⅔ cup: 87 cal., 4g fat (2g sat. fat), 9mg chol., 482mg sod., 12g carb. (5g sugars, 4g fiber), 4g pro. **Diabetic exchanges:** 1 vegetable, ½ starch, ½ fat.

MAPLE-GLAZED GREEN BEANS

After I picked my first green beans one year, I wanted to make a savory dish that was unique, quick, and packed with flavor. I loved this so much I couldn't stop eating it, so the next day I picked more beans and made this delicious side dish again.
—*Merry Graham, Newhall, CA*

TAKES: 25 MIN. • **MAKES:** 4 SERVINGS

- 3 cups cut fresh green beans
- 1 large onion, chopped
- 4 bacon strips, cut into 1-in. pieces
- ½ cup dried cranberries
- ¼ cup maple syrup
- ¼ tsp. salt
- ¼ tsp. pepper
- 1 Tbsp. bourbon, optional

1. In a large saucepan, place steamer basket over 1 in. of water. Place beans in basket. Bring water to a boil. Reduce heat to maintain a low boil; steam beans, covered, until crisp-tender, 4-5 minutes.
2. Meanwhile, in a large skillet, cook the onion and bacon over medium heat until bacon is crisp; drain. Stir cranberries, syrup, salt, pepper and, if desired, bourbon into onion mixture. Add beans; heat through, tossing to combine.
¾ cup: 173 cal., 3g fat (1g sat. fat), 7mg chol., 302mg sod., 35g carb. (24g sugars, 4g fiber), 4g pro.

SPINACH & TORTELLINI SOUP

A simple tomato-enhanced broth is perfect for cheese tortellini and fresh spinach. Increase the garlic and add Italian seasoning to suit your taste.
—Debbie Wilson, Burlington, NC

TAKES: 20 MIN. • MAKES: 6 SERVINGS (2 QT.)

- 1 tsp. olive oil
- 2 garlic cloves, minced
- 1 can (14½ oz.) no-salt-added diced tomatoes, undrained
- 3 cans (14½ oz. each) vegetable broth
- 2 tsp. Italian seasoning
- 1 pkg. (9 oz.) refrigerated cheese tortellini
- 4 cups fresh baby spinach
  Shredded Parmesan cheese
  Freshly ground pepper

1. In a large saucepan, heat oil over medium heat. Add garlic; cook and stir 1 minute. Stir in tomatoes, broth and Italian seasoning; bring to a boil. Add tortellini; bring to a gentle boil. Cook, uncovered, just until tortellini are tender, 7-9 minutes.
2. Stir in spinach. Sprinkle servings with cheese and pepper.
1⅓ **cups:** 164 cal., 5g fat (2g sat. fat), 18mg chol., 799mg sod., 25g carb. (4g sugars, 2g fiber), 7g pro.

EMILY'S HONEY LIME COLESLAW

Here's a refreshing take on slaw with a honey-lime vinaigrette rather than the traditional mayo. It's a fantastic take-along for all those summer picnics.
—Emily Tyra, Lake Ann, MI

PREP: 20 MIN. + CHILLING
MAKES: 8 SERVINGS

- 1½ tsp. grated lime zest
- ¼ cup lime juice
- 2 Tbsp. honey
- 1 garlic clove, minced
- ½ tsp. salt
- ¼ tsp. pepper
- ¼ tsp. crushed red pepper flakes
- 3 Tbsp. canola oil
- 1 small head red cabbage (about ¾ lb.), shredded
- 1 cup shredded carrots (about 2 medium carrots)
- 2 green onions, thinly sliced
- ½ cup fresh cilantro leaves

Whisk together the first 7 ingredients until smooth. Gradually whisk in oil until blended. Combine the cabbage, carrots and green onions; toss with lime mixture to lightly coat. Refrigerate, covered, 2 hours. Sprinkle with cilantro.
½ **cup:** 86 cal., 5g fat (0 sat. fat), 0 chol., 170mg sod., 10g carb. (7g sugars, 2g fiber), 1g pro. **Diabetic exchanges:** 1 vegetable, 1 fat.

GLAZED BABY CARROTS

For a zippy side dish, try this recipe. These brown sugar-glazed carrots come together in no time at all.
—Anita Foster, Fairmount, GA

TAKES: 15 MIN. • MAKES: 4 SERVINGS

- 1 lb. fresh, frozen or canned whole baby carrots
  Water
- 2 Tbsp. butter
- ¼ cup brown sugar

Cook the carrots in a small amount of water until tender. Drain. In a saucepan, combine butter and brown sugar; heat until sugar dissolves. Add carrots and toss to coat. Heat through.
¾ **cup:** 142 cal., 6g fat (4g sat. fat), 15mg chol., 152mg sod., 23g carb. (19g sugars, 2g fiber), 1g pro.

KITCHEN TIP: Dark brown sugar contains more molasses than light or golden brown sugar. The two types are generally interchangeable in recipes. If you prefer a bolder flavor, choose dark brown sugar.

SERVE WITH:
Peppery Roast Beef,
Page 31

GARDEN CHICKPEA SALAD

Looking for something different on a hot summer's day? This refreshing salad makes a terrific side or even an entree.

—*Sally Sibthorpe, Shelby Township, MI*

TAKES: 25 MIN. • **MAKES:** 2 SERVINGS

- ½ tsp. cumin seeds
- ¼ cup chopped tomato
- ¼ cup lemon juice
- ¼ cup olive oil
- 1 garlic clove, minced
- ¼ tsp. salt
- ¼ tsp. cayenne pepper

SALAD
- ¾ cup canned garbanzo beans or chickpeas, rinsed and drained
- 1 medium carrot, julienned
- 1 small zucchini, julienned
- 2 green onions, thinly sliced
- ½ cup coarsely chopped fresh parsley
- ¼ cup thinly sliced radishes
- ¼ cup crumbled feta cheese
- 3 Tbsp. chopped walnuts
- 3 cups spring mix salad greens

1. For dressing, in a dry small skillet, toast cumin seeds over medium heat until aromatic, stirring frequently. Transfer to a small bowl. Stir in the tomato, lemon juice, oil, garlic, salt and cayenne pepper.

2. In a bowl, combine the chickpeas, carrot, zucchini, green onions, parsley, radishes, cheese and walnuts. Stir in ⅓ cup dressing.

3. To serve, divide greens between 2 plates; top with chickpea mixture. Drizzle with remaining dressing.

1 serving: 492 cal., 38g fat (6g sat. fat), 8mg chol., 619mg sod., 30g carb. (7g sugars, 9g fiber), 12g pro.

GARDEN
CHICKPEA
SALAD

PARMESAN GARLIC BREADSTICKS

These tender breadsticks fill the kitchen with a tempting aroma when they are baking, and they're wonderful served warm. My family tells me I can't make them enough.

—*Gaylene Anderson, Sandy, UT*

PREP: 40 MIN. + RISING • **BAKE:** 10 MIN.
MAKES: 3 DOZEN

- 2 pkg. (¼ oz. each) active dry yeast
- 1½ cups warm water (110° to 115°)
- ½ cup warm 2% milk (110° to 115°)
- 3 Tbsp. sugar
- 3 Tbsp. plus ¼ cup butter, softened, divided
- 1 tsp. salt
- 4½ to 5½ cups all-purpose flour
- ¼ cup grated Parmesan cheese
- ½ tsp. garlic salt

1. In a large bowl, dissolve yeast in warm water. Add the milk, sugar, 3 Tbsp. butter, salt and 2 cups flour. Beat until smooth. Stir in enough remaining flour to form a soft dough.
2. Turn onto a floured surface; knead until smooth and elastic, 6-8 minutes. Place in a greased bowl, turning once to grease top. Cover and let rise in a warm place until doubled, about 45 minutes.
3. Punch the dough down. Turn onto a floured surface; divide into 36 pieces. Shape each piece into a 6-in. rope. Place 2 in. apart on greased baking sheets. Cover and let rise until doubled, about 25 minutes.
4. Melt remaining butter; brush over dough. Sprinkle with Parmesan cheese and garlic salt. Bake at 400° until golden brown, for 8-10 minutes. Remove from pans to wire racks.
1 breadstick: 86 cal., 3g fat (2g sat. fat), 7mg chol., 126mg sod., 13g carb. (1g sugars, 0 fiber), 2g pro.

DUTCH-OVEN BREAD

Crackling homemade bread makes an average day extraordinary. Enjoy this beautiful crusty bread recipe as is, or stir in a few favorites like cheese, garlic, herbs and dried fruits.

—*Catherine Ward, Mequon, WI*

PREP: 15 MIN. + RISING
BAKE: 45 MIN. + COOLING
MAKES: 1 LOAF (16 PIECES)

- 3 to 3½ cups (125 grams per cup) all-purpose flour
- 1 tsp. active dry yeast
- 1 tsp. salt
- 1½ cups water (70° to 75°)

1. In a large bowl, whisk 3 cups flour, yeast and salt. Stir in water and enough remaining flour to form a moist, shaggy dough. Do not knead. Cover and let rise in a cool place until doubled, 7-8 hours.
2. Preheat oven to 450°; place a Dutch oven with lid onto center rack and heat for at least 30 minutes. Once the Dutch oven is heated, turn the dough onto a generously floured surface. Using a metal scraper or spatula, quickly shape into a round loaf. Gently place on top of a piece of parchment.
3. Using a sharp knife, make a slash (¼ in. deep) across top of loaf. Using the parchment, immediately lower bread into heated Dutch oven. Cover; bake for 30 minutes. Uncover and bake until bread is deep golden brown and sounds hollow when tapped, 15-20 minutes longer, partially covering if browning too much. Remove loaf from pan and cool completely on wire rack.
1 slice: 86 cal., 0 fat (0 sat. fat), 0 chol., 148mg sod., 18g carb. (0 sugars, 1g fiber), 3g pro.

CHAPTER 5

TASTY ODDS & ENDS

Looking to make dinner extra special? Consider surprising your family with savory appetizers, sweet treats and everything in between. Whether you're rounding out a menu or simply need to bring a dish to pass, this enticing chapter has the answer.

SMOKY MACARONI & CHEESE

I found this recipe years ago in a magazine, and I just kept adding and subtracting ingredients until I found the perfect combination. You can make it in the oven, but grilling or smoking the dish is the real way to go.
—Stacey Dull, Gettysburg, OH

PREP: 40 MIN. • **GRILL:** 20 MIN. + STANDING
MAKES: 2 CASSEROLES (8 SERVINGS EACH)

- 6 cups small pasta shells
- 12 oz. Velveeta, cut into small cubes
- 2 cups shredded smoked cheddar cheese, divided
- 1 cup shredded cheddar cheese
- 1 cup 2% milk
- 4 large eggs, lightly beaten
- ¾ cup heavy whipping cream
- ⅔ cup half-and-half cream
- ½ cup shredded provolone cheese
- ½ cup shredded Colby-Monterey Jack cheese
- ½ cup shredded pepper jack cheese
- 1 tsp. salt
- ½ tsp. pepper
- ½ tsp. smoked paprika
  Optional: ½ tsp. liquid smoke, dash cayenne pepper and 8 bacon strips, cooked and crumbled

1. Preheat grill or smoker to 350°. Cook pasta according to package directions for al dente. Drain and transfer to a large bowl. Stir in Velveeta, 1 cup smoked cheddar, cheddar cheese, milk, eggs, heavy cream, half-and-half, provolone, Colby-Monterey Jack, pepper jack, salt, pepper, paprika, and, if desired, liquid smoke and cayenne pepper.
2. Transfer to 2 greased 13x9-in. baking pans; sprinkle with remaining 1 cup smoked cheddar cheese. Place on grill or smoker rack. Grill or smoke, covered, until a thermometer reads at least 160°, 20-25 minutes, rotating pans partway through cooking. Do not overcook. Let stand 10 minutes before serving; if desired, sprinkle with bacon.
1 cup: 403 cal., 23g fat (13g sat. fat), 117mg chol., 670mg sod., 30g carb. (4g sugars, 1g fiber), 18g pro.

APPETIZER TOMATO CHEESE BREAD

APPETIZER TOMATO CHEESE BREAD

I found this recipe in a dairy cookbook, and it has become a family favorite. We milk 180 cows and have a large garden, so we welcome dishes that use both dairy and fresh vegetables. My husband and our children are mostly meat-and-potato eaters, but I don't hear any complaints when I serve this irresistible bread!
—Penney Kester, Springville, NY

PREP: 20 MIN. • **BAKE:** 25 MIN. + STANDING
MAKES: 12 SERVINGS

- 2 Tbsp. butter
- 1 medium onion, minced
- 1 cup shredded cheddar cheese
- ½ cup sour cream
- ¼ cup mayonnaise
- ¾ tsp. salt
- ¼ tsp. pepper
- ¼ tsp. dried oregano
  Pinch rubbed sage
- 2 cups biscuit/baking mix
- ⅔ cup 2% milk
- 3 medium tomatoes, cut into ¼-in. slices
  Paprika

1. Preheat oven to 400°. In a small skillet, heat butter over medium heat. Add onion and cook until tender. Remove from the heat. Stir in the cheese, sour cream, mayonnaise and seasonings; set aside.
2. In a bowl, combine the baking mix and milk to form a soft dough. Turn dough onto a well-floured surface; knead lightly 10-12 times. Pat into a greased 13x9-in. baking dish, pushing dough up sides of dish to form a shallow rim. Arrange tomato slices over top. Spread with topping; sprinkle with paprika.
3. Bake for 25 minutes. Let stand for 10 minutes before cutting.
1 piece: 209 cal., 14g fat (6g sat. fat), 26mg chol., 521mg sod., 17g carb. (3g sugars, 1g fiber), 5g pro.

SERVE WITH:
Maple-Glazed Ham, Page 7

**CINNAMON
ALMOND
BRITTLE**

CHIP-CRUSTED GRILLED CORN

For my version of Mexican street corn, I roll the ears in crushed chips. For extra pizzazz, try different chip flavors such as ranch dressing and jalapeno.
—*Crystal Schlueter, Northglenn, CO*

TAKES: 30 MIN. • **MAKES:** 6 SERVINGS

- ¾ cup mayonnaise
- ¼ cup sour cream
- 2 Tbsp. minced fresh cilantro
- ½ tsp. salt
- ¼ tsp. cayenne pepper
- ¼ tsp. pepper
- 1 cup crushed tortilla chips
- 6 medium ears sweet corn, husks removed
  Lime wedges

1. In a small bowl, combine the first 6 ingredients. Refrigerate, covered, until serving. Place tortilla chips in a shallow bowl. Grill corn, covered, over medium heat 15-20 minutes or until tender, turning occasionally.
2. When cool enough to handle, spread corn with mayonnaise mixture; roll in chips. Grill corn, covered, 1-2 minutes longer or until lightly browned. Serve with lime wedges.
1 ear of corn: 355 cal., 27g fat (5g sat. fat), 17mg chol., 405mg sod., 26g carb. (7g sugars, 2g fiber), 4g pro.

KITCHEN TIP: This is messy (in the best way!) but can be made into a colorful, party-friendly dish with a few easy steps. Simply cut grilled corn off the cob, toss with the mayonnaise mixture and serve in portion cups topped with crushed chips and lime wedges. If you are sensitive to spice, omit the cayenne pepper or use sweet paprika instead.

CINNAMON ALMOND BRITTLE

It simply wouldn't be Christmas at our house without this old-time favorite twist on peanut brittle. No one believes how easy it is to make!
—*Lynette Kleinschmidt, Litchfield, MN*

PREP: 15 MIN. • **COOK:** 20 MIN. + COOLING
MAKES: ABOUT 2 LBS.

- 1 tsp. plus 3 Tbsp. butter, cubed
- 2 cups sugar
- ¾ cup light corn syrup
- ¼ cup water
- 3 cups slivered almonds, toasted
- 2 tsp. ground cinnamon
- ½ tsp. salt
- 1½ tsp. baking soda
- 1 tsp. vanilla extract

1. Preheat oven to 200°. Grease 2 baking sheets with 1 tsp. butter; place in oven to warm.
2. In a large heavy saucepan, combine sugar, corn syrup and water. Bring to a boil, stirring constantly to dissolve sugar. Using a pastry brush dipped in water, wash down the sides of the pan to eliminate sugar crystals. Cook, without stirring, over medium heat until a candy thermometer reads 240° (soft-ball stage). Stir in the almonds, cinnamon, salt and remaining butter; cook until thermometer reads 300° (hard-crack stage), stirring frequently and brushing sides of pan as needed.
3. Remove from heat; stir in baking soda and vanilla. Immediately pour onto prepared pans, spreading to ¼-in. thickness. Cool completely.
4. Break brittle into pieces. Store between layers of waxed paper in an airtight container.
1 oz.: 142 cal., 6g fat (1g sat. fat), 3mg chol., 111mg sod., 21g carb. (19g sugars, 1g fiber), 2g pro.

CHIP-CRUSTED
GRILLED CORN

BUTTERSCOTCH-RUM RAISIN TREATS

I love making rum raisin rice pudding, and those classic flavors inspired this treat. Crispy rice cereal adds crunch, but nuts, toasted coconut or candied pineapple could do the job, too.
—*Crystal Schlueter, Northglenn, CO*

TAKES: 20 MIN. • **MAKES:** ABOUT 4½ DOZEN

- 1 pkg. (10 to 11 oz.) butterscotch chips
- 1 pkg. (10 to 12 oz.) white baking chips
- ½ tsp. rum extract
- 3 cups Rice Krispies
- 1 cup raisins

1. Line 56 mini-muffin cups with paper liners. In a bowl, combine butterscotch and white chips. Microwave, uncovered, on high for 30 seconds; stir. Microwave in additional 30-second intervals, stirring until smooth.
2. Stir in extract, Rice Krispies and raisins. Drop by rounded tablespoonfuls into prepared mini muffin cups. Chill until set.
FREEZE OPTION: Freeze treats in freezer containers, separating layers with waxed paper. Thaw before serving.
1 treat: 76 cal., 4g fat (3g sat. fat), 1mg chol., 21mg sod., 11g carb. (9g sugars, 0 fiber), 0 pro.

HERBED FETA DIP

Guests can't get enough of this thick, zesty dip that bursts with fresh Mediterranean flavor. The feta cheese and fresh mint complement each other beautifully, creating the perfect sidekick for crunchy carrots, toasted pita chips, sliced baguettes or any other dipper you fancy.
—*Rebecca Ray, Chicago, IL*

TAKES: 25 MIN. • **MAKES:** 3 CUPS

- ½ cup packed fresh parsley sprigs
- ½ cup fresh mint leaves
- ½ cup olive oil
- 2 garlic cloves, peeled
- ½ tsp. pepper
- 4 cups (16 oz.) crumbled feta cheese
- 3 Tbsp. lemon juice
  Assorted fresh vegetables

In a food processor, combine the first 5 ingredients; cover and pulse until finely chopped. Add cheese and lemon juice; process until creamy. Serve with vegetables.
¼ cup: 176 cal., 15g fat (5g sat. fat), 20mg chol., 361mg sod., 2g carb. (0 sugars, 1g fiber), 7g pro.

WHITE ALMOND NO-BAKE COOKIES

My daughter and I like to try new recipes. We were out of chocolate chips one day, so we came up with this cookie using white chips.
—*Debbie Johnson, Winona Lake, IN*

PREP: 25 MIN. • **COOK:** 5 MIN. + CHILLING
MAKES: ABOUT 3½ DOZEN

- 2 cups sugar
- ½ cup butter, cubed
- ½ cup 2% milk
- 1 cup white baking chips
- ½ tsp. almond extract
- 3 cups old-fashioned oats
- 1 cup dried cherries or dried cranberries, optional

1. In a large saucepan, combine sugar, butter and milk. Cook and stir over medium heat until butter is melted and sugar is dissolved. Remove from heat. Stir in baking chips and extract until smooth. Add oats and, if desired, cherries; stir until coated.
2. Drop by rounded tablespoonfuls onto waxed paper-lined baking sheets. Refrigerate until set, about 30 minutes. Store cookies in an airtight container in the refrigerator.
1 cookie: 101 cal., 4g fat (2g sat. fat), 7mg chol., 23mg sod., 16g carb. (12g sugars, 1g fiber), 1g pro.

CREAMY CARAMEL MOCHA

Indulge in a coffeehouse-quality drink at Christmastime or any time at all. With whipped cream and a butterscotch drizzle, this mocha treat will perk up even the sleepiest person at the table.
—Taste of Home *Test Kitchen*

TAKES: 20 MIN. • **MAKES:** 6 SERVINGS

- ½ cup heavy whipping cream
- 1 Tbsp. confectioners' sugar
- 1 tsp. vanilla extract, divided
- ¼ cup Dutch-processed cocoa
- 1½ cups half-and-half cream
- 4 cups hot strong brewed coffee
- ½ cup caramel flavoring syrup
  Butterscotch-caramel
  ice cream topping

1. In a small bowl, beat the whipping cream until it begins to thicken. Add the confectioners' sugar and ½ tsp. vanilla; beat until stiff peaks form.
2. In a large saucepan over medium heat, whisk cocoa and half-and-half cream until smooth. Heat until bubbles form around sides of pan. Whisk in coffee, caramel syrup and remaining vanilla. Top servings with whipped cream; drizzle with butterscotch topping.
1 cup coffee with 2 Tbsp. whipped cream: 220 cal., 14g fat (9g sat. fat), 57mg chol., 38mg sod., 19g carb. (16g sugars, 1g fiber), 3g pro.

TO PREPARE IN A SLOW COOKER:
Prepare whipped cream as directed. Whisk together cocoa, half-and-half, coffee, caramel syrup and remaining vanilla in a 3-qt. slow cooker. Cook, covered, 2-3 hours or until heated through. Serve as directed.

SWEET ONION PIMIENTO CHEESE DEVILED EGGS

For my mother's 92nd birthday, we had deviled eggs topped with pimientos as part of the spread. They're timeless and always in good taste.
—Linda Foreman, Locust Grove, OK

TAKES: 15 MIN. • **MAKES:** 1 DOZEN

- 6 hard-boiled large eggs
- ¼ cup finely shredded sharp cheddar cheese
- 2 Tbsp. mayonnaise
- 4 tsp. diced pimientos, drained
- 2 tsp. finely chopped sweet onion
- 1 tsp. Dijon mustard
- 1 small garlic clove, minced
- ¼ tsp. salt
- ⅛ tsp. pepper
  Additional diced pimientos
  and finely shredded sharp
  cheddar cheese

Cut eggs lengthwise in half. Remove yolks, reserving whites. In a bowl, mash yolks. Stir in the cheese, mayonnaise, pimientos, onion, mustard, garlic, salt and pepper. Spoon or pipe mixture into egg whites. Sprinkle with additional pimientos and cheese. Refrigerate, covered, until serving.
1 stuffed egg half: 67 cal., 5g fat (2g sat. fat), 96mg chol., 128mg sod., 1g carb. (0 sugars, 0 fiber), 4g pro.

HOMEMADE CHURROS

These fried cinnamon-sugar goodies make a tasty dessert or fun snack.
—Taste of Home *Test Kitchen*

PREP: 15 MIN. + COOLING • **COOK:** 20 MIN.
MAKES: ABOUT 1 DOZEN

- ½ cup water
- ½ cup 2% milk
- 1 Tbsp. canola oil
- ¼ tsp. salt
- 1 cup all-purpose flour
- 1 large egg, room temperature
- ¼ tsp. grated lemon zest
  Additional oil for frying
- ½ cup sugar
- ¼ tsp. ground cinnamon

1. In a large saucepan, bring the water, milk, oil and salt to a boil. Add flour all at once and stir until a smooth ball forms. Transfer to a large bowl; let stand for 5 minutes.
2. Beat on medium-high speed for 1 minute or until the dough softens. Add egg and lemon zest; beat for 1-2 minutes. Set aside to cool.
3. In a deep cast-iron or heavy skillet, heat 1 in. oil to 375°. Insert a large star tip in a pastry bag; fill with dough. On a baking sheet, pipe dough into 4-in. strips.
4. Transfer strips to skillet and fry until golden brown on both sides. Drain on paper towels. Combine the sugar and cinnamon; sprinkle over churros. Serve churros warm.
1 fritter: 122 cal., 5g fat (1g sat. fat), 17mg chol., 60mg sod., 17g carb. (9g sugars, 0 fiber), 2g pro.

SOFT BEER
PRETZEL NUGGETS

FESTIVE CRANBERRY DRINK

Warm or cold? Take your choice of how to serve this colorful beverage. It's such a pretty color, and the spicy sweet-tart flavor is delightful with a meal or snack.
—Dixie Terry, Goreville, IL

PREP: 25 MIN. • **COOK:** 20 MIN. • **MAKES:** 3 QT.

- 4 cups fresh or frozen cranberries
- 3 qt. water, divided
- 1¾ cups sugar
- 1 cup orange juice
- ⅔ cup lemon juice
- ½ cup Red Hots
- 12 whole cloves

1. In a Dutch oven, combine cranberries and 1 qt. water. Cook over medium heat until berries pop, about 15 minutes. Remove from the heat. Strain through a fine strainer, pressing mixture with a spoon; discard skins. Return cranberry pulp and juice to the pan.
2. Stir in the sugar, juices, Red Hots and remaining water. Place cloves on a double thickness of cheesecloth. Bring up corners of cloth and tie with kitchen string to form a bag; add to juice mixture. Bring to a boil; cook and stir until sugar and Red Hots are dissolved.
3. Remove from heat. Strain through a fine mesh sieve or cheesecloth. Discard spice bag. Serve drink warm or cold.
1 cup: 178 cal., 0 fat (0 sat. fat), 0 chol., 1mg sod., 46g carb. (39g sugars, 2g fiber), 0 pro.

SOFT BEER PRETZEL NUGGETS

What goes together better than beer and pretzels? Not much that I can think of. That's why I put them together into one recipe. I'm always looking for new ways to combine fun flavors. I love the way this recipe turned out!
—Alyssa Wilhite, Whitehouse, TX

PREP: 1 HOUR + RISING
BAKE: 10 MIN./BATCH
MAKES: 8 DOZEN PRETZEL NUGGETS

- 1 bottle (12 oz.) amber beer or nonalcoholic beer
- 1 pkg. (¼ oz.) active dry yeast
- 2 Tbsp. unsalted butter, melted
- 2 Tbsp. sugar
- 1½ tsp. salt
- 4 to 4½ cups all-purpose flour
- 10 cups water
- ⅔ cup baking soda

TOPPING
- 1 large egg yolk
- 1 Tbsp. water
    Coarse salt, optional

1. In a small saucepan, heat beer to 110°-115°; remove from heat. Stir in yeast until dissolved. In a large bowl, combine butter, sugar, salt, yeast mixture and 3 cups flour; beat on medium speed until smooth. Stir in enough remaining flour to form a soft dough (dough will be sticky).
2. Turn dough onto a floured surface; knead it until smooth and elastic, 6-8 minutes. Place in a greased bowl, turning once to grease the top. Cover and let rise in a warm place until doubled, about 1 hour.
3. Preheat oven to 425°. Punch dough down. Turn onto a lightly floured surface; divide and shape into 8 balls. Roll each into a 12-in. rope. Cut each rope into 1-in. pieces.
4. In a Dutch oven, bring 10 cups water and baking soda to a boil. Drop nuggets, 12 at a time, into boiling water. Cook for 30 seconds. Remove with a slotted spoon; drain well on paper towels. Place on greased baking sheets. In a small bowl, whisk egg yolk and 1 Tbsp. water; brush over pretzels. Sprinkle with coarse salt if desired. Bake 10-12 minutes or until golden brown. Remove from pans to a wire rack to cool.

FREEZE OPTION: Freeze cooled pretzel nuggets in airtight containers. To use, thaw at room temperature or, if desired, microwave on high 20-30 seconds or until heated through.
6 pretzel nuggets: 144 cal., 2g fat (1g sat. fat), 8mg chol., 302mg sod., 26g carb. (2g sugars, 1g fiber), 4g pro.

KITCHEN TIP: To make pretzel rolls, divide and shape dough into 8 balls; roll each into a 14-in. rope. Starting at one end of each rope, loosely wrap dough around itself to form a coil. Boil, top and bake as directed. You can also make traditional pretzels with the same dough.

CINNAMON CHIP
CHAI-SPICED
SNICKERDOODLES

LEMON GELATO

On a recent trip to Italy, I became addicted to gelato. My favorite choice was lemon because Italian lemons have an intense flavor. This recipe brings back memories of our vacation.
—*Gail Wang, Troy, MI*

PREP: 30 MIN.
PROCESS: 20 MIN. + FREEZING
MAKES: 1½ QT.

- 1 cup whole milk
- 1 cup sugar
- 5 large egg yolks, lightly beaten
- 3 Tbsp. grated lemon zest
- ¾ cup fresh lemon juice (about 5 lemons)
- 2 cups heavy whipping cream

1. In a small heavy saucepan, heat milk to 175°; stir in sugar until dissolved. Whisk a small amount of hot mixture into egg yolks. Return all to the pan, whisking constantly. Add lemon zest. Cook over low heat until mixture is just thick enough to coat a metal spoon and a thermometer reads at least 160°, stirring constantly. Do not allow to boil.
2. Remove immediately from heat; stir in lemon juice and cream. Place in a bowl. Press plastic wrap onto the surface of the custard; refrigerate several hours or overnight.
3. Fill cylinder of ice cream freezer two-thirds full; freeze according to the manufacturer's directions. (Refrigerate remaining mixture until ready to freeze.) Transfer ice cream to freezer containers, allowing headspace for expansion. Freeze 2-4 hours or until firm. Repeat with remaining mixture.
⅔ cup: 361 cal., 26g fat (15g sat. fat), 213mg chol., 40mg sod., 31g carb. (27g sugars, 0 fiber), 4g pro.

CINNAMON CHIP CHAI-SPICED SNICKERDOODLES

I love cinnamon chips, and this is an intriguing way to use them. Make sure to stock up on them during the holiday season so you have plenty to last throughout the year.
—*Marietta Slater, Justin, TX*

PREP: 30 MIN. + CHILLING
BAKE: 15 MIN./BATCH + COOLING
MAKES: ABOUT 6 DOZEN

- ½ cup sugar
- 2 tsp. ground cardamom
- 2 tsp. ground cinnamon
- ½ tsp. ground ginger
- ½ tsp. ground cloves
- ¼ tsp. ground nutmeg

DOUGH
- ½ cup butter, softened
- ½ cup shortening
- 1 cup sugar
- 2 large eggs, room temperature
- 1 tsp. vanilla extract
- 2¾ cups all-purpose flour
- 2 tsp. cream of tartar
- 1 tsp. baking soda
  Dash salt
- 1 pkg. (10 oz.) cinnamon baking chips

1. Preheat oven to 350°. For spiced sugar, mix first 6 ingredients.
2. In a large bowl, cream butter, shortening, sugar and 2 Tbsp. spiced sugar until light and fluffy. Beat in eggs and vanilla. In another bowl, whisk together flour, cream of tartar, baking soda and salt; gradually beat into creamed mixture. Stir in baking chips. Refrigerate, covered, until firm enough to shape, about 1 hour.
3. Shape dough into 1-in. balls; roll in remaining spiced sugar. Place 2 in. apart on greased baking sheets.
4. Bake until set, 11-13 minutes. Remove from pans to wire racks to cool.
1 cookie: 81 cal., 4g fat (2g sat. fat), 9mg chol., 59mg sod., 10g carb. (7g sugars, 0 fiber), 1g pro.

OLD-FASHIONED
FRUIT COMPOTE

OLD-FASHIONED FRUIT COMPOTE

This warm and fruity side dish can simmer on its own while you prepare the rest of your menu, or make it a day ahead and reheat it before serving.

—*Shirley Glaab, Hattiesburg, MS*

PREP: 15 MIN. • **COOK:** 1 HOUR
MAKES: 8 CUPS

- 1 can (20 oz.) pineapple chunks, undrained
- 1 can (15¼ oz.) sliced peaches, undrained
- 1 can (11 oz.) mandarin oranges, undrained
- 1 pkg. (18 oz.) pitted dried plums (prunes)
- 2 pkg. (3½ oz. each) dried blueberries
- 1 pkg. (6 oz.) dried apricots
- ½ cup golden raisins
- 4 lemon zest strips
- 1 cinnamon stick (3 in.)
- 1 jar (10 oz.) maraschino cherries, drained

Drain pineapple, peaches and oranges, reserving the juices; set drained fruit aside. In a Dutch oven, combine fruit juice, dried fruits, lemon zest strips and cinnamon stick. Bring to a boil. Reduce heat; cover and simmer until dried fruit is tender, about 30 minutes. Add reserved canned fruit and cherries; heat just until warmed through. Serve warm or at room temperature.
¼ cup: 126 cal., 0 fat (0 sat. fat), 0 chol., 4mg sod., 31g carb. (22g sugars, 2g fiber), 1g pro.

SERVE WITH:
Juicy Roast Turkey,
Page 15

SPICY POTATOES
WITH GARLIC AIOLI

SPICY POTATOES WITH GARLIC AIOLI

This is my take on Spanish patatas bravas. The potatoes are tossed in a flavorful spice mix and then finished to a crispy golden brown. The garlic aioli takes it over the top for an unconventional potato salad that'll be a hit at any party.

—*John Stiver, Bowen Island, BC*

PREP: 35 MIN. • **BAKE:** 25 MIN.
MAKES: 10 SERVINGS (1¾ CUPS AIOLI)

- 3 lbs. medium Yukon Gold potatoes, cut into 1½-in. cubes (about 8 potatoes)
- 2 Tbsp. olive oil
- 2 garlic cloves, minced
- 2 Tbsp. smoked paprika
- 2 tsp. garlic powder
- 1½ tsp. chili powder
- 1½ tsp. ground cumin
- ¼ tsp. salt
- ¼ tsp. crushed red pepper flakes
- ⅛ tsp. pepper

AIOLI
- 1½ cups mayonnaise
- 3 Tbsp. lemon juice
- 3 garlic cloves, minced
- 1 Tbsp. minced fresh chives plus additional for topping
- 1 tsp. red wine vinegar
- ¼ tsp. salt
- ¼ tsp. pepper

1. Preheat oven to 375°. Place potatoes in a Dutch oven; add water to cover. Bring to a boil. Reduce heat; cook, uncovered, 8-10 minutes or until just tender. Drain; pat dry with paper towels. Transfer potatoes to a mixing bowl. Toss the potatoes in oil and minced garlic to coat evenly.
2. Combine the paprika, garlic powder, chili powder, cumin, salt, pepper flakes and pepper; sprinkle over potatoes. Gently toss to coat. Transfer potatoes to 2 greased 15x10x1-in. baking pans, spreading into a single layer. Bake until crispy, about 25 minutes, stirring the potatoes and rotating pans halfway through cooking.
3. For aioli, combine ingredients until blended. Transfer potatoes to a serving platter; sprinkle with chives. Serve warm with aioli.
¾ cup potatoes with about 3 Tbsp. aioli: 469 cal., 34g fat (5g sat. fat), 3mg chol., 396mg sod., 37g carb. (3g sugars, 4g fiber), 5g pro.

KITCHEN TIP: The seasoning blend gives these potatoes a nice kick; smoked paprika makes them taste as if they were cooked over an open fire. Remember this spice mix the next time you're prepping Tater Tots, and sprinkle some on for an instant upgrade.

CHAPTER 6
MEMORY-MAKING DESSERTS

Few things top off family dinners like a lip-smacking sweet. From cakes layered with flavor to pies bursting with berry goodness, homemade desserts steal the show at Sunday dinners, holiday parties and casual get-togethers alike. Turn here for the impressive specialties that will earn you a blue ribbon from family and friends.

EASY NUTELLA CHEESECAKE

A creamy chocolate-hazelnut spread tops a crust made of crushed Oreo cookies to make this irresistible baked cheesecake.
—*Nick Iverson, Denver, CO*

PREP: 35 MIN. • **BAKE:** 1¼ HOURS + CHILLING
MAKES: 16 SERVINGS

- 2½ cups lightly crushed Oreo cookies (about 24 cookies)
- ¼ cup sugar
- ¼ cup butter, melted

FILLING
- 4 pkg. (8 oz. each) cream cheese, softened
- ½ cup sugar
- 2 jars (26½ oz. each) Nutella
- 1 cup heavy whipping cream
- 1 tsp. salt
- 4 large eggs, room temperature, lightly beaten
- ½ cup chopped hazelnuts, toasted

1. Preheat oven to 325°. Pulse cookies and sugar in a food processor until fine crumbs form. Continue processing while gradually adding the butter in a steady stream. Press mixture onto bottom of a greased 10x3-in. springform pan. Securely wrap bottom and side of springform in a double thickness of heavy-duty foil (about 18 in. square).
2. For filling, beat cream cheese and sugar until smooth. Beat in the Nutella, cream and salt. Add eggs; beat on low speed just until blended. Pour over crust.
3. Bake until a thermometer inserted in center reads 160°, about 1¼ hours. Cool 1¼ hours on a wire rack. Refrigerate cheesecake overnight, covering when completely cooled.
4. Gently loosen side from pan with a knife; remove rim. Top cheesecake with chopped hazelnuts.
1 piece: 900 cal., 62g fat (22g sat. fat), 129mg chol., 478mg sod., 84g carb. (71g sugars, 4g fiber), 12g pro.

LEMON-LIME BARS

LEMON-LIME BARS

I baked these bars for a luncheon, and a gentleman made his way to the kitchen to compliment the cook who made them.
—*Holly Wilkins, Lake Elmore, VT*

PREP: 20 MIN. • **BAKE:** 20 MIN. + COOLING
MAKES: 4 DOZEN

- 1 cup butter, softened
- ½ cup confectioners' sugar
- 2 tsp. grated lime zest
- 1¾ cups all-purpose flour
- ¼ tsp. salt

FILLING
- 4 large eggs, room temperature
- 1½ cups sugar
- ¼ cup all-purpose flour
- ½ tsp. baking powder
- ⅓ cup lemon juice
- 2 tsp. grated lemon zest
  Confectioners' sugar

1. Preheat oven to 350°. In a large bowl, cream butter and confectioners' sugar until light and fluffy. Beat in lime zest. Combine flour and salt; gradually add to creamed mixture and mix well.
2. Press into a greased 13x9-in. baking dish. Bake just until edges are lightly browned, 13-15 minutes.
3. Meanwhile, in another large bowl, beat eggs and sugar. Combine flour and baking powder. Gradually add to egg mixture. Stir in lemon juice and zest; beat until frothy. Pour over hot crust.
4. Bake until light golden brown, 20-25 minutes. Cool on a wire rack. Dust with confectioners' sugar. Cut into squares. Store in the refrigerator.
1 bar: 88 cal., 4g fat (2g sat. fat), 28mg chol., 60mg sod., 12g carb. (7g sugars, 0 fiber), 1g pro.

KITCHEN TIP: When zesting limes or lemons, remember that the outermost part of a citrus fruit has the most desirable flavor. Be careful not to grate too far down into the peel. The lighter-colored inner part of the peel, the pith, tastes bitter.

STRAWBERRY-CHOCOLATE MERINGUE TORTE

SANDY'S CHOCOLATE CAKE

Years ago, I drove four hours to a cake contest, holding my entry on my lap the whole way. But it paid off. One bite and you'll see why this velvety beauty was named the best chocolate cake recipe and won first prize.
—Sandy Johnson, Tioga, PA

PREP: 30 MIN. • **BAKE:** 30 MIN. + COOLING
MAKES: 16 SERVINGS

- 1 cup butter, softened
- 3 cups packed brown sugar
- 4 large eggs, room temperature
- 2 tsp. vanilla extract
- 2⅔ cups all-purpose flour
- ¾ cup baking cocoa
- 3 tsp. baking soda
- ½ tsp. salt
- 1⅓ cups sour cream
- 1⅓ cups boiling water

FROSTING
- ½ cup butter, cubed
- 3 oz. unsweetened chocolate, chopped
- 3 oz. semisweet chocolate, chopped
- 5 cups confectioners' sugar
- 1 cup sour cream
- 2 tsp. vanilla extract

STRAWBERRY-CHOCOLATE MERINGUE TORTE

I make this rich and delicious torte whenever I'm asked to bring dessert to any occasion. You can use reduced-calorie whipped topping if you'd like to create a lighter version.
—Christine McCullough, Auburn, MA

PREP: 45 MIN. • **BAKE:** 70 MIN. + COOLING
MAKES: 6 SERVINGS

- 4 large egg whites
- 3 cups sliced fresh strawberries
- 1 tsp. plus 1 cup sugar, divided
- 1½ cups heavy whipping cream
- ⅓ cup confectioners' sugar
- ¾ tsp. vanilla extract
- ¼ tsp. cream of tartar
- ¼ tsp. salt
- ½ cup semisweet chocolate chips

1. Place egg whites in a large bowl; let stand at room temperature 30 minutes. Meanwhile, in a small bowl, combine strawberries and 1 tsp. sugar. In another bowl, beat cream until it begins to thicken. Add confectioners' sugar and vanilla; beat until soft peaks form. Refrigerate strawberries and whipped cream, covered, until assembly.
2. Preheat oven to 250°. Line a baking sheet with parchment. Trace two 8-in. circles 1 in. apart on paper. Add cream of tartar and salt to egg whites; beat on medium speed until foamy. Gradually add remaining 1 cup sugar, 1 Tbsp. at a time, beating on high after each addition until sugar is dissolved. Continue beating until stiff glossy peaks form. Spread evenly over circles.
3. Bake until set and dry, 70-80 minutes. Turn off oven (do not open oven door); leave meringues in oven 1½ hours. Remove from oven; cool completely.
4. In a microwave, melt chocolate chips; stir until smooth. Spread evenly over tops of meringues. Carefully remove 1 meringue to a serving plate. Remove whipped cream from refrigerator; beat until stiff peaks form. Spread half of the whipped cream over the meringue; top with half of the strawberries. Repeat layers. Serve immediately.
1 piece: 470 cal., 26g fat (16g sat. fat), 68mg chol., 154mg sod., 58g carb. (54g sugars, 2g fiber), 5g pro.

1. Preheat oven to 350°. Grease and flour three 9-in. round baking pans.
2. In a large bowl, cream the butter and brown sugar until light and fluffy, 5-7 minutes. Add eggs, 1 at a time, beating well after each addition. Beat in vanilla. In another bowl, whisk flour, cocoa, baking soda and salt; add to creamed mixture alternately with sour cream, beating well after each addition. Stir in boiling water until blended.
3. Transfer to prepared pans. Bake the layers until a toothpick comes out clean, 30-35 minutes. Cool in pans 10 minutes; remove to wire racks to cool completely.
4. For the frosting, in a metal bowl over simmering water, melt butter and both chocolates; stir until smooth. Cool mixture slightly.
5. In a large bowl, combine the confectioners' sugar, sour cream and vanilla. Add chocolate mixture; beat until smooth. Spread frosting between the layers and over top and side of cake. Refrigerate leftovers.
1 piece: 685 cal., 29g fat (18g sat. fat), 115mg chol., 505mg sod., 102g carb. (81g sugars, 3g fiber), 7g pro.

SANDY'S
CHOCOLATE CAKE

BLACKBERRY CRISP

I adapted this comforting dessert from a recipe my mother-in-law gave me. Hers fed a family with nine growing kids who were never full, so there was never any left. When I make my downsized version, there are never any leftovers either!
—Marliss Lee, Independence, MO

PREP: 15 MIN. • **BAKE:** 20 MIN.
MAKES: 2 SERVINGS

- 2 cups fresh or frozen blackberries
- 2 Tbsp. sugar
- 1 tsp. cornstarch
- 1½ tsp. water
- ½ tsp. lemon juice
- ½ cup quick-cooking oats
- ¼ cup all-purpose flour
- ¼ cup packed brown sugar
- ½ tsp. ground cinnamon
- ¼ cup cold butter
  Vanilla ice cream

1. Place blackberries in a greased 1-qt. baking dish. In a small bowl, combine the sugar, cornstarch, water and lemon juice until smooth. Pour over berries. Combine oats, flour, brown sugar and cinnamon; cut in butter until crumbly. Sprinkle over the berries.
2. Bake, uncovered, at 375° until filling is bubbly, 20-25 minutes. Serve warm with ice cream.
1¼ cups: 576 cal., 25g fat (14g sat. fat), 61mg chol., 245mg sod., 87g carb. (54g sugars, 6g fiber), 6g pro.

CAST-IRON
PEACH CROSTATA

CAST-IRON PEACH CROSTATA

While the crostata, an open-faced fruit tart, is actually Italian, my version's peach filling is American all the way.
—Lauren McAnelly, Des Moines, IA

PREP: 45 MIN. + CHILLING • **BAKE:** 45 MIN.
MAKES: 10 SERVINGS

- 1½ cups all-purpose flour
- 2 Tbsp. plus ¾ cup packed brown sugar, divided
- 1¼ tsp. salt, divided
- ½ cup cold unsalted butter, cubed
- 2 Tbsp. shortening
- 3 to 5 Tbsp. ice water
- 8 cups sliced peaches (about 7-8 medium)
- 1 Tbsp. lemon juice
- 3 Tbsp. cornstarch
- ½ tsp. ground cinnamon
- ¼ tsp. ground nutmeg
- 1 large egg, beaten
- 2 Tbsp. sliced almonds
- 1 Tbsp. coarse sugar
- ⅓ cup water
- 1 cup fresh raspberries, optional

1. Mix flour, 2 Tbsp. brown sugar and 1 tsp. salt; cut in butter and shortening until crumbly. Gradually add ice water, tossing with a fork until dough holds together when pressed. Shape into a disk. Cover and refrigerate 1 hour or overnight.
2. Combine peaches and lemon juice. Add remaining ¾ cup brown sugar, cornstarch, spices and remaining ¼ tsp. salt; toss gently. Let stand 30 minutes.
3. Preheat oven to 400°. On a lightly floured surface, roll dough into a 13-in. circle; transfer to a 10-in. cast-iron skillet, letting excess hang over edge. Using a slotted spoon, transfer peaches into crust, reserving liquid. Fold crust edge over filling, pleating as you go, leaving center uncovered. Brush folded crust with beaten egg; sprinkle with almonds and coarse sugar. Bake until crust is dark golden and filling bubbly, 45-55 minutes.
4. In a small saucepan, combine the reserved liquid and water; bring to a boil. Simmer until thickened, 1-2 minutes; serve warm with pie. If desired, top with fresh raspberries.
1 piece: 322 cal., 13g fat (7g sat. fat), 43mg chol., 381mg sod., 49g carb. (30g sugars, 3g fiber), 4g pro.

STRAWBERRY
MASCARPONE CAKE

STRAWBERRY MASCARPONE CAKE

This cake bakes up high and fluffy, and the berries add a fresh fruity flavor.
—*Carol Wit, Tinley Park, IL*

PREP: 1 HOUR + CHILLING
BAKE: 30 MIN. + COOLING
MAKES: 12 SERVINGS

- 6 cups fresh strawberries, halved (2 lbs.)
- 2 Tbsp. sugar
- 1 tsp. grated orange zest
- 1 Tbsp. orange juice
- ½ tsp. almond extract

CAKE
- 6 large eggs, separated, room temperature
- 2 cups cake flour
- 2 tsp. baking powder
- ¼ tsp. salt
- 1½ cups sugar, divided
- ½ cup canola oil
- ¼ cup water
- 1 Tbsp. grated orange zest
- ½ tsp. almond extract

WHIPPED CREAM
- 2 cups heavy whipping cream
- ⅓ cup confectioners' sugar
- 2 tsp. vanilla extract

FILLING
- 1 cup mascarpone cheese
- ½ cup heavy whipping cream

1. In a large bowl, combine the first 5 ingredients. Refrigerate, covered, at least 30 minutes. Meanwhile, place egg whites in a large bowl; let stand at room temperature 30 minutes. Preheat oven to 350°. Grease bottoms of two 8-in. round baking pans; line with parchment. Sift the flour, baking powder and salt together twice; place in another large bowl.

2. In a small bowl, whisk egg yolks, 1¼ cups sugar, oil, water, orange zest and almond extract until blended. Add to flour mixture; beat until well blended.

3. With clean beaters, beat egg whites on medium speed until soft peaks form. Gradually add remaining ¼ cup sugar, 1 Tbsp. at a time, beating on high after each addition until sugar is dissolved. Continue beating until soft glossy peaks form. Fold a fourth of the egg whites into batter, then fold in remaining whites.

4. Gently transfer to prepared pans. Bake on lowest oven rack until the top springs back, 30-35 minutes. Cool in pans 10 minutes before removing to wire racks; remove paper. Cool completely.

5. Meanwhile, for whipped cream, in a large bowl, beat cream until it begins to thicken. Add confectioners' sugar and vanilla; beat until soft peaks form. Refrigerate, covered, at least 1 hour. For filling, in a small bowl, beat mascarpone cheese and cream until stiff peaks form. Refrigerate until assembling.

6. Drain strawberries, reserving juice mixture. Using a serrated knife, trim tops of cakes if domed. Place 1 cake layer on a serving plate. Brush with half of reserved juice mixture; spread with ¾ cup of the filling. Arrange half of the strawberries over top, creating an even layer; spread with remaining filling. Brush remaining cake layer with the remaining juice mixture; place layer over filling, brushed side down.

7. Gently stir whipped cream; spread over top and side of cake. Just before serving, arrange remaining strawberries over cake.

1 piece: 677 cal., 48g fat (22g sat. fat), 196mg chol., 200mg sod., 56g carb. (36g sugars, 2g fiber), 10g pro.

APPLE BUTTER CAKE ROLL

This spicy gingerbread cake is a new take on a classic pumpkin roll. It might make you think back fondly to your grandma's Christmas cookies.

—Debbie White, Williamson, WV

PREP: 35 MIN. • **BAKE:** 15 MIN. + CHILLING
MAKES: 15 SERVINGS

- 3 large eggs, separated
- 1 cup all-purpose flour, divided
- 2 Tbsp. plus ½ cup sugar, divided
- 2 tsp. ground cinnamon
- 1 tsp. baking powder
- 1 tsp. ground ginger
- 1 tsp. ground cloves
- ¼ tsp. baking soda
- ¼ cup butter, melted
- ¼ cup molasses
- 2 Tbsp. water
- 1 Tbsp. confectioners' sugar
- 2 cups apple butter

1. Preheat oven to 375°. Place egg whites in a small bowl; let stand at room temperature for 30 minutes. Line a greased 15x10x1-in. baking pan with waxed paper and grease the paper. Sprinkle with 1 Tbsp. flour and 2 Tbsp. sugar; set aside.
2. In a large bowl, combine remaining flour and ½ cup sugar; add the cinnamon, baking powder, ginger, cloves and baking soda. In another bowl, whisk the egg yolks, butter, molasses and water. Add to dry ingredients and beat until blended. Beat egg whites on medium speed until soft peaks form; fold into batter. Pour into prepared pan.
3. Bake for 12-14 minutes or until the cake springs back when lightly touched. Cool for 5 minutes. Turn cake onto a kitchen towel dusted with confectioners' sugar. Gently peel off waxed paper. Roll up cake in the towel jelly-roll style, starting with a short side. Cool completely on a wire rack.
4. Unroll cake; spread apple butter to within ½ in. of edges. Roll up again. Cover and chill for 1 hour before serving. Refrigerate leftovers.

1 piece: 186 cal., 4g fat (2g sat. fat), 45mg chol., 100mg sod., 35g carb. (26g sugars, 1g fiber), 2g pro. **Diabetic exchanges:** 2 starch, 1 fat.

SERVE WITH:
Autumn Apple
Chicken, Page 60

CHOCOLATE PECAN SKILLET COOKIE

Bake up the ultimate shareable cookie. For variety, swap out the chocolate chips for an equal quantity of M&M's or chocolate chunks. Or go super fancy by mixing the chocolate chips and pecans into the dough, then gently folding in 1½ cups fresh raspberries.
—*James Schend, Pleasant Prairie, WI*

PREP: 15 MIN. • **BAKE:** 35 MIN.
MAKES: 12 SERVINGS

- 1   **cup butter**
- 1   **cup sugar**
- 1   **cup packed brown sugar**
- 2   **large eggs, room temperature**
- 2   **tsp. vanilla extract**
- 3   **cups all-purpose flour**
- 1½ **tsp. baking soda**
- ½   **tsp. kosher salt**
- 1   **cup 60% cacao bittersweet chocolate baking chips**
- 1   **cup chopped pecans, toasted Vanilla ice cream, optional**

1. Preheat oven to 350°. In a 12-in. cast-iron skillet, heat butter in oven as it preheats. Meanwhile, in a large bowl, stir together sugar and brown sugar. When butter is almost melted, remove skillet from oven and swirl butter until completely melted. Stir butter into sugar mixture; set skillet aside.
2. Beat eggs and vanilla into the sugar mixture. In another bowl, whisk together flour, baking soda and salt; gradually beat into sugar mixture. Stir in chocolate chips and nuts. Spread mixture into buttered skillet.
3. Bake until toothpick inserted in center comes out with moist crumbs and top is golden brown, 35-40 minutes. Serve warm, with vanilla ice cream if desired.
1 serving: 528 cal., 27g fat (13g sat. fat), 72mg chol., 378mg sod., 69g carb. (43g sugars, 3g fiber), 6g pro.

KITCHEN TIP: This cookie may be prepared in four 6-in. cast-iron skillets. Just brush skillets with melted butter before adding dough. Bake for 25-30 minutes. For a dairy-free option, substitute shortening or nondairy margarine for the butter.

CHOCOLATE PECAN SKILLET COOKIE

BANANA PUDDING

I didn't see my son for more than two years after he enlisted in the Marines after high school. And when I saw him arrive at the airport, I just grabbed hold of him and burst out crying. When we got home, the first thing he ate was two bowls of my easy banana pudding. He's a true southern boy! It's a dessert, but you can have it for breakfast, lunch or dinner.
—*Stephanie Harris, Montpelier, VA*

PREP: 35 MIN. + CHILLING
MAKES: 9 SERVINGS

- ¾ cup sugar
- ¼ cup all-purpose flour
- ¼ tsp. salt
- 3 cups 2% milk
- 3 large eggs
- 1½ tsp. vanilla extract
- 8 oz. vanilla wafers (about 60 cookies), divided
- 4 large ripe bananas, cut into ¼-in. slices

1. In a large saucepan, mix sugar, flour and salt. Whisk in milk. Cook and stir over medium heat until thickened and bubbly. Reduce heat to low; cook and stir 2 minutes longer. Remove from heat.
2. In a small bowl, whisk the eggs. Whisk a small amount of hot mixture into the eggs; return all to the pan, whisking constantly. Bring to a gentle boil; cook and stir 2 minutes. Remove from heat. Stir in vanilla. Cool for 15 minutes, stirring occasionally.
3. In an ungreased 8-in. square baking dish, layer 25 vanilla wafers, half of the banana slices and half of the pudding. Repeat layers.
4. Press plastic wrap onto surface of pudding. Refrigerate for 4 hours or overnight. Just before serving, remove wrap; crush remaining wafers and sprinkle over top.
1 serving: 302 cal., 7g fat (2g sat. fat), 80mg chol., 206mg sod., 55g carb. (37g sugars, 2g fiber), 7g pro.

KITCHEN TIP: Use plastic wrap over the pudding to prevent a skin from forming. The plastic peels off easily after the pudding cools.

BANANA PUDDING

MIXED FRUIT SHORTCAKES

This delightful downsized recipe makes just two biscuit-like shortcakes. You can fill them with the fresh fruit of your choice and top with whipped cream for an impressive dinner finale.
—Sue Ross, Casa Grande, AZ

TAKES: 30 MIN. • **MAKES:** 2 SERVINGS

- 1 cup mixed fresh berries
- ½ cup sliced fresh peaches or nectarines
- 4 tsp. sugar, divided
- ½ cup all-purpose flour
- ¾ tsp. baking powder
- ⅛ tsp. salt
- 2 Tbsp. shortening
- 3 Tbsp. 2% milk
  Whipped cream

1. In a small bowl, combine the berries, peaches and 2 tsp. sugar. In another bowl, combine the flour, baking powder and salt; cut in shortening until mixture is crumbly. Stir in the milk just until moistened. Drop dough by lightly packed ⅓ cupfuls 2 in. apart onto an ungreased baking sheet. Gently flatten into 2½-in. circles. Sprinkle with remaining sugar.
2. Bake at 425° for 10-12 minutes or until golden brown. Remove to a wire rack to cool. Split the shortcakes horizontally in half. Spoon fruit onto bottoms; spread whipped cream over fruit or on the shortcake tops.
1 serving: 329 cal., 13g fat (3g sat. fat), 2mg chol., 311mg sod., 48g carb. (20g sugars, 5g fiber), 5g pro.

CARAMEL FLUFF & TOFFEE TRIFLE

The best part of this stunning layered dessert is that you need just five ingredients to put it together.
—Daniel Anderson, Kenosha, WI

PREP: 15 MIN. + CHILLING
MAKES: 12 SERVINGS

- 2 cups heavy whipping cream
- ¾ cup packed brown sugar
- 1 tsp. vanilla extract
- 1 prepared angel food cake (8 to 10 oz.), cut into 1-in. cubes
- 1 cup milk chocolate English toffee bits

1. In a large bowl, beat cream, brown sugar and vanilla just until blended. Refrigerate, covered, 20 minutes. Beat until stiff peaks form.
2. In a 4-qt. glass bowl, layer one-third of each of the following: cake cubes, whipped cream and toffee bits. Repeat layers twice. Refrigerate until serving.
1 serving: 347 cal., 22g fat (13g sat. fat), 61mg chol., 227mg sod., 38g carb. (27g sugars, 0 fiber), 2g pro.

SERVE WITH:
Chicken Marsala
Lasagna, Page 49

BERRY-PATCH BROWNIE PIZZA

I just love the combination of fruit, almonds and chocolate that makes this brownie unique. The fruit lightens the chocolate a bit and makes it feel as though you are eating something sinfully healthy.
—*Sue Kauffman, Columbia City, IN*

PREP: 20 MIN. + CHILLING
BAKE: 15 MIN. + COOLING
MAKES: 12 SERVINGS

  1 **pkg. fudge brownie mix
     (13x9-in. pan size)**
  ⅓ **cup chopped unblanched almonds**
  1 **tsp. almond extract**
TOPPING
  1 **pkg. (8 oz.) cream cheese, softened**
  1 **Tbsp. sugar**
  1 **tsp. vanilla extract**
  ½ **tsp. grated lemon zest**
  2 **cups whipped topping
     Assorted fresh berries
     Optional: Fresh mint leaves and
     coarse sugar**

1. Preheat oven to 375°. Prepare brownie batter according to package directions for fudgelike brownies, adding almonds and almond extract. Spread batter into a greased 14-in. pizza pan.
2. Bake until a toothpick inserted in the center comes out clean, 15-18 minutes. Cool completely on a wire rack.
3. Beat first 4 topping ingredients until smooth; fold in whipped topping. Spread over crust to within ½ in. of edges; refrigerate, loosely covered, 2 hours.
4. To serve, cut into 12 wedges; top with berries of choice. If desired, top with mint and sprinkle with coarse sugar.
1 piece: 404 cal., 26g fat (8g sat. fat), 51mg chol., 240mg sod., 39g carb. (26g sugars, 2g fiber), 5g pro.

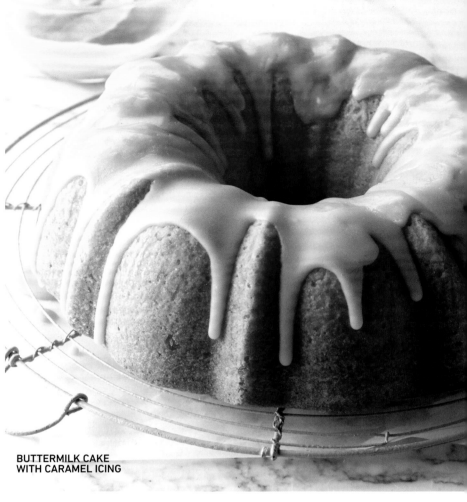

BUTTERMILK CAKE
WITH CARAMEL ICING

BUTTERMILK CAKE WITH CARAMEL ICING

So moist and tender, this cake melts in your mouth! It's been a favorite cake recipe of my family since the 1970s and goes over really well at potlucks and bake sales.
—*Anna Jean Allen, West Liberty, KY*

PREP: 35 MIN. • **BAKE:** 45 MIN. + COOLING
MAKES: 16 SERVINGS

  1 **cup butter, softened**
  2⅓ **cups sugar**
  1½ **tsp. vanilla extract**
  3 **large eggs, room temperature**
  3 **cups all-purpose flour**
  1 **tsp. baking powder**
  ½ **tsp. baking soda**
  1 **cup buttermilk**
ICING
  ¼ **cup butter, cubed**
  ½ **cup packed brown sugar**
  ⅓ **cup heavy whipping cream**
  1 **cup confectioners' sugar**

1. Preheat oven to 350°. Grease and flour a 10-in. fluted tube pan.
2. Cream butter and sugar until light and fluffy, 5-7 minutes. Beat in vanilla and 1 egg at a time, beating well after each addition. In another bowl, whisk together flour, baking powder and baking soda; add to creamed mixture alternately with buttermilk (batter will be thick). Transfer to prepared pan.
3. Bake until a toothpick inserted in center comes out clean, 45-50 minutes. Cool in pan 10 minutes before removing to a wire rack to cool completely.
4. For the icing, in a small saucepan, combine the butter, brown sugar and cream; bring to a boil over medium heat, stirring constantly. Remove from heat; cool 5-10 minutes. Gradually beat in confectioners' sugar; spoon over cake.
1 piece: 419 cal., 17g fat (11g sat. fat), 79mg chol., 230mg sod., 63g carb. (44g sugars, 1g fiber), 4g pro.

KITCHEN TIP: To remove cakes easily, use solid shortening to grease plain and fluted tube pans.

BLUEBERRY
DREAM PIE

to prevent overbrowning. Cool on a wire
rack. Refrigerate leftovers.

1 piece: 442 cal., 18g fat (8g sat. fat), 46mg
chol., 269mg sod., 67g carb. (35g sugars,
3g fiber), 5g pro.

PASTRY FOR DOUBLE-CRUST PIE (9 IN.)
Mix 2½ cups all-purpose flour and ½ tsp.
salt; cut in 1 cup cold butter until crumbly.
Gradually add ⅓ to ⅔ cup ice water,
tossing with a fork until dough holds
together when pressed. Divide dough in
half. Shape each into a disk; cover and
refrigerate 1 hour or overnight.

BERRY BLISS COBBLER

A little bit sweet, a little bit tart and topped
off with golden sugar-kissed biscuits, this
cobbler is summer perfection.
—Taste of Home *Test Kitchen*

PREP: 10 MIN. + STANDING • **BAKE:** 20 MIN.
MAKES: 6 SERVINGS

  3 cups fresh strawberries, halved
1½ cups fresh raspberries
1½ cups fresh blueberries
  ⅔ cup plus 1 Tbsp. sugar, divided
  3 Tbsp. quick-cooking tapioca
  1 cup all-purpose flour
      2 tsp. baking powder
  ¼ tsp. salt
  ¼ cup cold butter, cubed
  1 large egg, room temperature
  ¼ cup plus 2 Tbsp. 2% milk
      Coarse sugar

1. Preheat oven to 400°. Toss the
strawberries, raspberries and
blueberries with ⅔ cup sugar and
tapioca. Transfer to a greased 10-in.
cast-iron or other ovenproof skillet;
let stand 20 minutes.
2. Meanwhile, whisk flour, remaining
1 Tbsp. sugar, baking powder and salt.
Cut in butter until mixture resembles
coarse crumbs. In another bowl, whisk
together egg and milk; stir into crumb
mixture just until moistened. Drop by
tablespoonfuls onto fruit. Sprinkle with
coarse sugar.
3. Bake, uncovered, until the filling is
bubbly and topping is golden brown,
20-25 minutes. Serve warm.

1 serving: 335 cal., 9g fat (5g sat. fat), 56mg
chol., 298mg sod., 60g carb. (34g sugars,
5g fiber), 5g pro.

BLUEBERRY DREAM PIE

This showstopping pie can be decorated
to fit any season or holiday. I like to make
stars for Independence Day, leaves for fall,
hearts for Valentine's Day or even flowers
for spring. Have fun with it!
—Kerry Nakayama, New York, NY

PREP: 40 MIN. • **BAKE:** 35 MIN. + COOLING
MAKES: 8 SERVINGS

    Dough for double-crust pie
CHEESE FILLING
  4 oz. reduced-fat cream cheese
  ½ cup confectioners' sugar
  1 Tbsp. lemon juice
  1 large egg yolk, room temperature
BLUEBERRY FILLING
  ½ cup plus 1 Tbsp. sugar, divided
  2 Tbsp. all-purpose flour
  1 Tbsp. cornstarch
  ¼ cup cold water
  6 cups fresh or frozen blueberries,
      divided
  2 Tbsp. lemon juice
  1 Tbsp. minced fresh mint or 1 tsp.
      dried mint
  1 large egg white, beaten

1. On a floured surface, roll each dough
disk to fit a 9-in. deep-dish cast-iron or
other cast-iron skillet. Line skillet with
bottom crust. Trim crust to ½ in. beyond
edge of pan; flute edges. Line the
unpricked crust with a double thickness
of heavy-duty foil. Bake at 450° for
8 minutes. Remove foil; bake 5 minutes
longer. Cool on a wire rack. Reduce heat
to 375°.
2. In a small bowl, beat the cream
cheese, confectioners' sugar and lemon
juice until light and fluffy. Beat in egg
yolk until blended. Spread into crust.
3. In a large saucepan, combine ½ cup
sugar, flour and cornstarch; stir in water
until smooth. Stir in 2 cups berries. Bring
to a boil; cook and stir until thickened,
1-2 minutes. Cool slightly. Gently stir
in the lemon juice, mint and remaining
4 cups berries. Pour over cheese filling.
4. Cut decorative cutouts from remaining
crust; arrange over filling, leaving center
uncovered. Brush crust with egg white;
sprinkle with remaining 1 Tbsp. sugar.
5. Bake pie at 375° until the crust is
golden brown and filling is bubbly,
35-40 minutes. If necessary, cover the
edges with foil during the last 15 minutes

RECIPE INDEX

A

Agua de Jamaica, 28
Almond Broccoli Salad, 16
Appetizer Tomato Cheese Bread, 89
Apple Barbecue Chicken, 64
Apple Butter Cake Roll, 106
Apple Roasted Pork
    with Cherry Balsamic Glaze, 64
Apple & Walnut Stuffed Pork Tenderloin
    with Red Currant Sauce, 66
Autumn Apple Chicken, 60
Autumn Apple Torte, 20

B

Baked Beans Mole, 80
Balsamic Braised Pot Roast, 57
Banana Pudding, 108
Beef & Bacon Gnocchi Skillet, 50
Beef Tenderloin with
    Roasted Vegetables, 67
Berry Bliss Cobbler, 111
Berry-Patch Brownie Pizza, 110
Best-Ever Fried Chicken, 11
Biltmore's Bread Pudding, 32
Blackberry Crisp, 104
Blueberry Dream Pie, 111
Broccoli Beer Cheese Soup, 19
Buttermilk Cake with Caramel Icing, 110
Butternut Harvest Pies, 36
Butterscotch-Rum Raisin Treats, 92

C

Caramel Fluff & Toffee Trifle, 109
Caraway Cheese Bread, 20
Carrot Blueberry Cupcakes, 44
Cast-Iron Peach Crostata, 104
Cheese & Garlic Biscuits, 44
Chicken & Goat Cheese Skillet, 63
Chicken Marsala Lasagna, 49
Chicken-Stuffed Cubanelle Peppers, 62
Chip-Crusted Grilled Corn, 90
Chipotle Citrus-Glazed Turkey Tenderloins, 60
Chive Smashed Potatoes, 78
Chocolate & Coconut Cream Torte, 8
Chocolate Pecan Skillet Cookie, 107
Cider-Glazed Ham, 62
Cinnamon Almond Brittle, 90
Cinnamon Chip Chai-Spiced Snickerdoodles, 95
Citrus-Herb Roast Chicken, 71
Citrus-Tarragon Asparagus Salad, 7
Country-Fried Steak, 63
Creamy Caramel Mocha, 93
Creamy Root Veggie Soup, 81
Crunchy Coated Walleye, 62

D

Dutch-Oven Bread, 85

E

Easy Batter Rolls, 76
Easy Nutella Cheesecake, 101
Eddie's Favorite Fiesta Corn, 27
Emily's Honey Lime Coleslaw, 83

F

Favorite Chocolate-Bourbon Pecan Tart, 24
Festive Cranberry Drink, 94
Frogmore Stew, 23

G

Garden Chickpea Salad, 84
Garlic-Herb Pattypan Squash, 35
Glazed Baby Carrots, 83
Glazed Smoked Chops with Pears, 51
Grandma's Swedish Meatballs, 69
Green Salad with Berries, 43
Grilled Ribeyes with Browned Garlic Butter, 63

H

Herbed Feta Dip, 92
Herbed Harvest Vegetable Casserole, 79
Herb Quick Bread, 82
Homemade Churros, 93

I

Individual Shepherd's Pies, 55
Italian Cream Cheese Cake, 40
Italian Pinwheel Rolls, 40

J

Juicy Roast Turkey, 15

K

Kale Caesar Salad, 12

L

Lemon Gelato, 95
Lemon-Lime Bars, 101

M

Maple-Glazed Green Beans, 82
Maple-Glazed Ham, 7
Meatball Chili with Dumplings, 71
Mixed Fruit Shortcakes, 109
Moist Turkey Sausage Stuffing, 15
Mom's Sweet Potato Bake, 76

N

New England Bean & Bog Cassoulet, 56

O

Old-Fashioned Fruit Compote, 97
Old-World Rye Bread, 36
Onion & Green Chile Enchiladas, 27
Oven-Fried Cornbread, 23
Overnight Yeast Rolls, 8

P

Parmesan Garlic Breadsticks, 85
Peach-Glazed Ribs, 69
Peppery Roast Beef, 31
Pork Shepherd's Pie, 35
Pretzel-Crusted Catfish, 68
Puff Pastry Chicken Potpie, 52
Pumpkin & Cauliflower Garlic Mash, 82

R

Ravioli with Creamy Squash Sauce, 50
Raw Cauliflower Tabbouleh, 32
Red & Green Salad with Toasted Almonds, 78
Red, White & Blue Summer Salad, 75
Refreshing Raspberry Iced Tea, 8
Risotto Balls (Arancini), 39
Roasted Apple Salad with
    Spicy Maple-Cider Vinaigrette, 19
Roasted Red Pepper Green Beans, 31

S

Salmon with Root Vegetables, 57
Sandy's Chocolate Cake, 102
Sausage Lasagna, 39
Sausage & Squash Penne, 51
Shrimp Puttanesca, 56
Simple Au Gratin Potatoes, 75
Sliced Ham with Roasted Vegetables, 52
Slow-Cooked Beef Brisket, 65
Slow-Cooked Pork Stew, 49
Smoky Grilled Pizza with Greens & Tomatoes, 54
Smoky Macaroni & Cheese, 89
Soft Beer Pretzel Nuggets, 94
Southern Buttermilk Biscuits, 12
Southern Sweet Potato Tart, 16
Spicy Pork & Green Chili Verde, 28
Spicy Potatoes with Garlic Aioli, 97
Spinach & Tortellini Soup, 83
Strawberry-Chocolate Meringue Torte, 102
Strawberry Mascarpone Cake, 105
Sweet Onion Pimiento Cheese Deviled Eggs, 93
Sweet Tea Boysenberry Shandy, 24

T

Tamale Pie, 51
Tilapia with Corn Salsa, 50
Traditional Mashed Potatoes, 12
Turkey Curry with Rice, 65
Tuscan Fish Packets, 43

W

White Almond No-Bake Cookies, 92

Z

Zucchini in Dill Cream Sauce, 79